ANGLESEY

160 pages of (

BEST

Editor: Osian Pennant Hughes

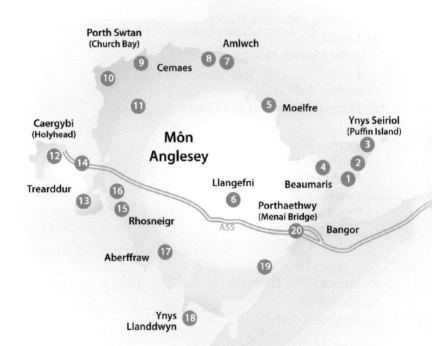

Porth Swtan
(Church Bay)

Amlwch

⑨ Cemaes ⑧ ⑦

⑩

⑪

⑤ Moelfre

Caergybi
(Holyhead)

Môn
Anglesey

Ynys Seiriol
(Puffin Island)

③

⑫

②

⑭

④

①

Trearddur

Llangefni

Beaumaris

⑯

⑥

⑬

Porthaethwy
(Menai Bridge)

⑮

Rhosneigr

A55

⑳

Bangor

Aberffraw ⑰

⑲

Ynys ⑱
Llanddwyn

Contents

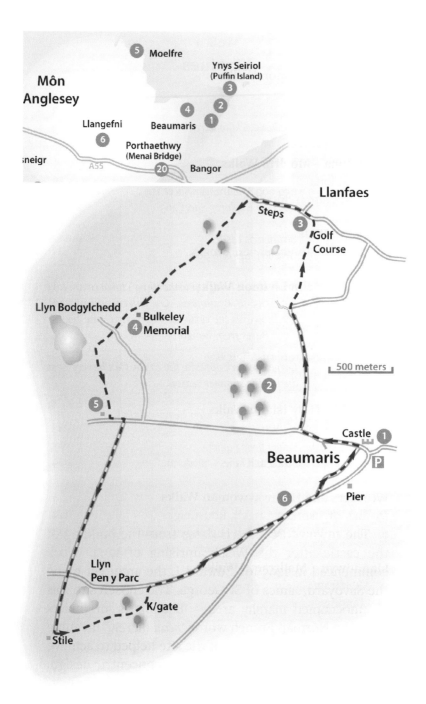

Walk 1
Llanfaes

Walk details
Approx distance: *6 miles/9.6 kilometres*

Approx time:	*3 hours*
O.S. Maps:	*1:50 000 Landranger Sheet 114* *1:25 000 Explorer Sheet 263*
Start:	*Beaumaris castle* *Grid Ref. SH 606 762*
Access:	*From Menai Bridge (Porthaethwy) town centre take the A545 to Beaumaris. On entering Beaumaris, head towards the castle and turn right into the car park. Buses from Bangor.*
Parking:	*Large car park opposite the castle. Can be very busy during the summer season.*
Please note:	*Fields can be wet after heavy rainfall.*
Going:	*Valley floor / quiet.* *Fields and lanes – moderate.*

Points of Interest
1. The town of Beaumaris dates from the building of the castle after the Welsh uprising of 1294. Work commenced in 1295 for Edward I, the architect being the Savoyard, James of St George. The chosen site was an unoccupied marshy area – 'Beaumaris' originates from the Norman French words *'beau mareys'* meaning 'fair marsh'. The levelness of the site helped to achieve the plan of a perfectly symmetrical, concentric design.

Beaumaris castle and moat

A channel linked the moat surrounding the castle to the sea. However, money ran out and the structure was never completed. It lacks the high towers and battlements of fortresses such as Harlech and Conwy. This was the last of the castles built by Edward I to occupy the independent kingdom of Gwynedd. Welsh families from Llanfaes were evicted to Rhosyr, which became known as Newborough (*Niwbwrch*). Meanwhile, having acquired its biased marketing benefits, the colonial town of Beaumaris grew and prospered.

2. The now derelict Baron Hill mansion was the seat of the Williams-Bulkeley family. William Bulkeley came from Cheshire about 1440 when he was made Constable of the Castle. He married into an important local family and acquired much land. The tomb of William Bulkeley and his wife Elen is in the parish church. They built a town house in Beaumaris,

Henblas, which, regretably, was demolished in 1869. Later members of the Bulkeley family built the first Baron Hill mansion in 1618, and it was rebuilt in 1776 by Samuel Wyatt, a renowned architect. Further alterations were carried out about 150 years ago. In the Second World War it was a camp for the Royal Welch Fusiliers and a military hospital. Unoccupied since then, it is now a ruin and surrounded by trees. On his visit to Baron Hill, Pennant noted that the coffin of Siwan, Princess Joan, was in use as a horse watering trough. After being rescued, the coffin was displayed in a mausoleum in the grounds of Baron Hill. It is now in the porch of the parish church. The Bulkeley line passed to the Williams-Bulkeleys in 1822.

3. Formerly owned by the Hampton family, the building of Henllys Hall functioned as a monastery for 20 years before becoming a hotel in 1971. The medieval town of Llanfaes was probably situated where the modern village is now. Before Beaumaris was built, it was an important commercial centre and a major European port for the Welsh princes. No traces remain of the friary founded in 1237 by Llywelyn Fawr (*Llywelyn the Great*) in honour of his wife Siwan. The site is near the coast under fields and factory grounds. Siwan, Princess Joan, Llywelyn's wife and King John's illegitimate daughter, was buried at the Franciscan Friary, her body transported across the Lavan Sands (*Traeth Lafan*). Other important ladies of Gwynedd were buried there, including Senena, Llywelyn's mother and Eleanor de Montfort, wife of Llywelyn ap Gruffudd. After the Dissolution of the Monasteries, during the reign of Henry VIII, the cover stone of Siwan's coffin was taken to Beaumaris church.

4. The impressive Bulkeley Memorial, built of Penmon marble, was erected in 1876 in honour of a Sir Richard who died the previous year, aged 73. The history of the family has some dramatic events. In 1624, a Sir Richard Bulkeley died of suspected poisoning; there was evidence of arsenic or a similar poison in his tobacco. His widow soon married Thomas Cheadle who had worked for the family. However, the pair were not brought for trial until 1634. They were found Not Guilty because although there was strong evidence against them, it was not infallible. There was proof that poison was bought but not when and the servant responsible for mixing the tobacco died before the date of the trial. Sir Richard left a son, another Sir Richard, who wanted revenge.

5. The Almshouses were built in 1613. They were paid for through the will of David Hughes who also founded a free grammar school in the town. Red Hill, the hill south-east of here, was the site of a battle during the 2nd Civil War. The Royalist Constable, a Colonel Richard Bulkeley, lost the castle to Parliamentary forces in 1646. The islanders revolted and during the Battle of Beaumaris (1648) on Red Hill about 30-40 lives were lost on each side.

6. Before the building of the Menai Bridge in 1826 ferries transported people across the Strait. One of the earliest ferries went to Llanfaes, later it switched to The Green at Beaumaris. On the route for Ireland, Beaumaris became a post town and boats carried horses as well as people. The crossing of Lavan Sands was only safe in 3 or 4 hours out of every 12. Old charts

The stone cask of Siwan, Llywelyn's wife, at Beaumaris church

show two routes – one passed below Penmaen Mawr, the other farther west. The Corporation paid for posts to be erected across the sands to guide people to the ferry. In later years the ferry terminal moved to Gallows Point (*Penrhyn Safnes*) then stopped altogether about 1830. It was on Lavan Sands that the Bulkeley-Cheadle feud came to an end. After the Civil Wars young Colonel Bulkeley travelled abroad. On his return, whilst on the sands, he met Richard Cheadle who had helped Parliamentary troops cross the Strait. They fought a duel and Bulkeley was slain. Cheadle was hanged at Conwy. About the time of the last ferries excursion boats from Liverpool started to call at Beaumaris. The Victorian pier was longer than it is now. *La Marguerite*, a paddle-steamer belonging to the Liverpool and North Wales Steamship Company, could carry over 2000 passengers.

Walk directions   **(-) denotes Point of Interest**
From the castle entrance (1) take the road leaving the main street and pass the castle on your right. At the Catholic Church turn right along Rating Row to a road junction. Turn right past a pub, the Sailor's Return.

Take the lane signposted to Henllys Hotel. Pass Baron Hall East Lodge on the left (2).

At the driveway for the hotel bear right with the lane. In a few paces turn left on a footpath.

Follow the footpath onto a golf course. Keep ahead aiming towards the white house at the

The Public Footpath whilst crossing the Henllys Hotel Golf Course

far end (don't turn right) to a kissing gate and lane (3).

Turn left and, in a short distance, left again uphill. Do not take the first signposted footpath sign. Shortly after the lane starts to descend, go up steps on the left to a stile and footpath.

On reaching a field keep ahead by the left boundary to a small footbridge. Continue uphill to a bench – a good place for a break to enjoy the views.

Go over the stile and turn right. Then aim upwards to the next stile – taking care whilst crossing the golf course. Head now towards the Bulkeley Memorial (4). Look back for fine views as far as the Great Orme at Llandudno. Before the monument climb a ladder stile and continue to the lane.

Cross the lane to another footpath. Follow the hedge on the right to the corner of the field and a view of Llyn Bodgylched. Turn left and descend the fields to a stile and lane by the Almshouses (5).

Turn left and take the next lane right. Cross over a crossroads and follow the winding lane past Llyn Pen-y-parc. Where the lane bends right, turn left over a stone stile.

Keep ahead, bearing slightly left downhill. Before a building on the right, swing left and go through a gap in the wall between a gatepost and gorse bush.

Take the path through the trees and bushes to a footpath signpost. Continue to a low post. At a fork take the left-hand path to a kissing gate and field. Keep ahead to another kissing gate and lane.

Turn right, downhill, to the road bordering the Menai Strait (6). Turn left into Beaumaris.

Facilities
All facilities available in Beaumaris. Public toilets are at the start, near the castle. Camp site at Llanfaes. Many interesting buildings in the town including the Tudor Rose, a medieval hall house. Boat trips from the pier.

Originally published in
Circular Walks on Anglesey

by Dorothy Hamilton

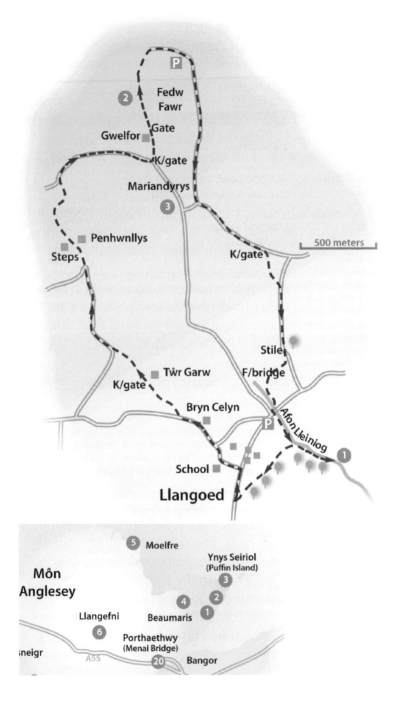

Walk 2
Llangoed

Walk details
Approx distance: *6 miles/9.6 kilometres*

Approx time: *2½ hours*

O.S. Maps: *1:50 000 Landranger Sheet 114*
1:25 000 Explorer Sheet 263

Start: *Llangoed Village*
Grid Ref. SH 611 797

Access: *From Menai Bridge (Porthaethwy) town centre take*
the A545 to Beaumaris. Continue on the B5109 to
Llangoed. Buses from Bangor and Menai Bridge.

Parking: *Large free car park by the old bridge in Llangoed*
village.

Please note: *Fields can be rather wet after heavy rainfall.*

Going: *Lanes / quiet.*
Paths, fields and lanes – moderate.

Points of Interest
1. A low motte, Castell Aber Lleiniog, is on the opposite side of the river. During the Norman invasion the Earl of Chester built a timber castle on this man-made mound but it was soon captured by the Welsh under Gruffudd ap Cynan. In the 17th century Thomas Cheadle, who had married Richard Bulkeley's widow (see Walk 1: Llanfaes, Point of Interest 4), built a stone fort on the site. It became known as 'Lady Cheadle's

The stone cask of Siwan, Llywelyn's wife, at Beaumaris church

Fort'. Thomas Cheadle turned traitor during the Civil War and offered the castle to Parliament. Royalists intercepted the letter and he was incarcerated in Beaumaris dungeon. Later, the fort was used by seamen from Parliamentary ships in the Strait. The small, square castle, now a ruin, had a turret at each corner. To continue on the walk, return to the track.

2. This is Fedw Fawr, a 45-acre common owned by the National Trust, which is one of the few breeding sites for black guillemots. Fulmars, razorbills and gulls also nest on the limestone cliffs. There are extensive views along the coast and out to Puffin Island (*Ynys Seiriol*) and the Great Orme. Yellowhammers, stonechats, blackcaps and whitethroats may be seen or heard on the heath and scrubland. In summer the heath is colourful with flowers – bell heather, saw-wort, kidney vetch, mountain everlasting and various orchids.

3. From this point it is only a few minutes walk to the Mariandyrys Nature Reserve, which is cared for by the North Wales Wildlife Trust. The reserve is just 15 acres of common land, a hill of carboniferous limestone covered by heather, gorse and grassland. Linnets and dunnocks nest and the reserve is especially attractive to butterflies such as the grayling, brown argus, small tortoiseshell and painted lady. Plants include the common rockrose, burnet saxifrage and a number of orchids. To visit the reserve, turn right on the lane and at a T-junction cross the stile to the left of the house opposite. A path climbs the hill, crossing a track, to an area of grassland from where there are fine views over the surrounding countryside. To continue on the walk, return to * and keep ahead on the lane.

Walk directions (-) denotes Point of Interest
Cross the little bridge over Afon Lleiniog and immediately bear right. Turn right at a fork and follow the river until the track veers left to a gate. Keep ahead on the woodland path for about 150 metres (1).

A very detailed information board outlining the history of Llangoed, which is situated in the car park at the start of the walk

Retrace your steps to the track. After a few more metres bear left on grass just before a house. Follow the left banking and continue on a path. At a junction of paths bear left to meet a road.

Turn right and in about 200 metres turn left on a road. Pass a school and ignore a lane on the right into a housing estate, and ignore the next right turn as well. Pass a house called Bryn Celyn and take the next lane right.

At the farm called Tŵr Garw keep ahead and go through a kissing gate. Continue by the left edge of fields until a kissing gate gives access to a lane.

Turn right on the lane. When it bends left keep ahead on the track for Penhwnllys Plas. At the farm gate follow the new diversion up steps on the left and continue to a field. (If the diversion is not yet in place go through the gate and cross the farmyard to the field.)

Keep ahead by the left edge of the field to a kissing gate. Continue through similar gates, bearing right and then left on an enclosed path which leads to a lane.

Bear right and in 800 metres go through a kissing gate on the left beside the drive for Gwelfor. Continue by the hedge on the right when the drive leaves it. Pass a house on the left and reach an enclosed path which leads to a gate. Take a path slanting left to join a wide path and follow it towards the sea (2).

After exploring Fedw Fawr take a path to the small car park and follow the narrow lane to a T-junction (3).

Bear left to return to Llangoed (*). The lane goes past a few houses and rises between walls. Opposite a track on the left turn right through a kissing gate.

The path descends through gorse and crosses an open field. Go uphill to have a cemetery on the right. Turn right on the lane.

Pass a school and continue another 500 metres to a stile on the right. Follow the left edge of the field and turn left over a footbridge to a kissing gate.

Go past a cottage and follow the drive to a road. Turn right to the car park at the start.

Facilities
Small car park at Fedw Fawr. Pub near end of walk.

Originally published in
Circular Walks on Anglesey

by Dorothy Hamilton

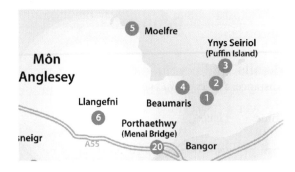

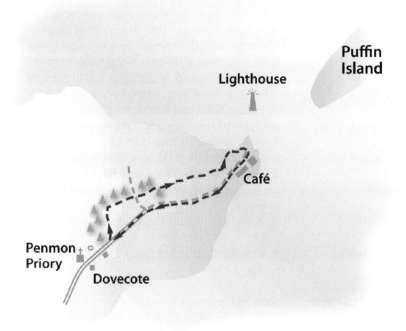

Walk 3

Penmon

Walk details

Approx distance: *2 miles/3.2 kilometres*

Approx time: *1 hour*

O.S. Maps: *1:50 000 Landranger Sheet 114*
                1:25 000 Explorer Sheet 263

Start: *Penmon Priory*
                Grid Ref. SH 631 808

Access: *Drive straight through Beaumaris and continue on this road, passing Beaumaris castle on your left, as the road becomes the B5109 to Llangoed. Approximately 2½ miles/4 km after passing the castle, you reach a crossroads of two minor roads. Take the turning on the right, signposted to Penmon. Follow this minor road, taking care at some of the very sharp bends and narrow stretches, for about 3 miles/4.8 km, until you reach the ruins of Penmon Priory. To follow the walk, park here and follow the walking directions to Penmon. Alternatively, if you do not wish to walk at all, you can drive right out to the Point itself. In either case, a small fee is payable in season.*
                Turn right towards Penmon from the B5109.

Parking: *A large car park near Penmon Priory. There is a parking fee.*

Please note: *Some wet ground – especially in the field leading from the lane towards the pine trees.*

Going: *Quiet.*
                Field, coast and small lanes.

Walk description

This is an excellent walk which can be enjoyed at any time of year, though it may be rather blowy in winter. You will follow paths across a mixture of farmland and heathland out to the coast itself, and be rewarded with fine views of the Anglesey coastline and Puffin Island (*Ynys Seiriol*), as well as the north coast of the mainland and the mountains of Eryri/Snowdonia. The bushes lining the fields and dotted about the heathland provide shelter for smaller resident birds and migrants in spring and autumn, while time spent sea-watching at the point itself is likely to give you excellent views of seabirds and mammals in this beautiful setting. Add a sprinkling of culture in the form of Penmon Priory ruins, and a friendly café to restore you at the furthest point on your walk, and what more could you ask!

Walk directions

If you have parked beside Penmon Priory, it is worth taking a look at the historic buildings before setting off on your walk.

There is said to have been a monastery here since the 6th century, founded by St Seiriol, but most evidence was destroyed by Viking raids. In the 12th century, the priory church was rebuilt, and is still in use today. In the 13th century, Penmon became a more substantial Augustinian priory, but it was dissolved in 1538. The land and buildings were acquired by the Bulkeley family from Beaumaris, who also built the square dovecote around 1600 to house around a thousand doves in cubby holes in the walls.

Penmon priory

Opposite the dovecote, take the footpath signposted St Seiriol's Well, passing the monks' fishpond on your right.

You can sometimes see Brown Trout in this pool, and a family party of Moorhens is usually in residence, while dragonflies skim the water in summer. Check the bushes overhanging the water for Willow Warblers, members of the tit family, House Sparrows and finches, while in summer Swallows may swoop over the water to snatch a drink or scoop up hovering insects. Continuing on to the site of St Seiriol's Well, the original well is supposed to date from the 6th century, although the upper building around it was built in the 18th century.

Retrace your steps back to the dovecote and turn left to walk uphill up the lane. Passing a cottage to your right, you reach a field entrance to your left where you should climb over the stile into the field. Continue forwards across the field heading for a wall and a stand of pine trees on the far side. Head towards the gate on the left side of the trees, and after passing through it you will see a small kissing gate on your right leading into the pine trees. Bear right and follow along beside the bushes at the edge of the field. This section can sometimes be a little soggy underfoot.

As you walk along, check all the bushes and trees carefully for sheltering birds such as Chaffinches, Greenfinches, Goldfinches, Bullfinches, Willow Warblers, Chiffchaffs, Common Whitethroats and Goldcrests. Look up and you may see a raptor overhead: Buzzards are sometimes seen circling, or if you are lucky, a Peregrine may chase through.

At the end of the field, you reach a small lane. Turn right and then immediately left at the footpath signs, to follow another path along the edge of the next field, again checking the bushes for birds as you go. Go through the kissing gate

and continue along the footpath through a little copse of small trees and scrubby bush. This section can be rather muddy, so do take care. You emerge from this copse into a more open area of heathland and bracken with willows, hawthorn, rowan, sloes and blackberry bushes dotted about.

This stile takes you through a very pleasant wooded area

Again this is a good area to see warblers such as

Chiffchaffs and Willow Warblers, so it is worth checking all the bushes carefully, stopping to both look and listen.

As you round a bend, you get your first view of Puffin Island and the lighthouse of Penmon, and hear the mournful clang of its bell. Follow the steps downhill, and at the brow of the small hill, the path splits, with the right-hand path heading straight towards the Coastguards' Cottages. Take the left-hand path which winds its way down to the shoreline before heading towards the cottages on the Point.

As you walk along, check the shoreline for Oystercatchers, Turnstones, and other shore waders. At the Point itself, it is worth taking the time to sit and do a spot of sea-watching.

Looking across to Puffin Island, you are likely to see roosts of Cormorants, Guillemots and Razorbills on the island or on the water, and a small number of Puffins, though these are easier to see with a telescope. In summer, keep an eye out for other seabirds such as Sandwich Terns and Gannets passing through between their breeding colonies and fishing sites, as well as various gulls, and duck such as Common Scoter and Eider. You may be lucky enough to see Grey Seals keeping a curious eye on the human activity, and Harbour Porpoise and Dolphin have also been seen here.

One of the Pilot's Cottages here has been converted into a café, providing a welcome pit-stop before the walk back.
    To return to your car, follow the narrow lane for about

Penmon and Ynys Seiriol (Puffin Island) across the strait

a mile back to the Priory, ignoring any side turnings. It is worth taking the time to check the bushes on either side of the road for a last chance to see more passerines.

What to look for ...
... in summer: If you look with binoculars out from the Point towards Puffin Island you should see seabirds such as Fulmars, Kittiwakes, Guillemots, Razorbills, Gannets and Sandwich Terns flying past, and if you are lucky maybe a Puffin too. Of course, a telescope will give you much better views of these sometimes distant birds. The bushes beside the path and dotted over the heathland are the best place to look for Common and Lesser Whitethroats, Blackcaps, Chiffchaffs, Willow Warblers and Sedge Warblers, though you may see warblers in the bushes around the fishpond too.

... in winter: Looking off the Point, you may see Red-throated Divers, Great Crested Grebes and Red-breasted Mergansers on the water

... all year round: Check the large rocks on the shoreline for Cormorants and Shags gathering, while Oystercatchers and Rock Pipits may be busy on the smaller stones by the water's edge. Stonechats and Meadow Pipits may sit up on the heathland bushes, and don't forget to look upwards: Peregrines, Buzzards, Ravens and even Choughs may be flying overhead.

Where to eat
The Pilot House Café, in a converted lighthouse pilot's cottage at Penmon, offers hot and cold drinks and snacks, ices and homemade cakes. The café is open daily from 9 a.m. – 6 p.m. in summer, and during

Black Guillemot

daylight hours at the weekends only in winter. You may wish to call to check opening hours on 07776 006804.

Other information
- Parking available at Penmon Priory and at the far end of Penmon.
- Parking fee payable in season for either parking site.
- No public toilets; toilets at café for customers only.
- Use of a telescope will give much better views of passing seabirds from Penmon.

On your drive to or from Penmon, you may wish to stop at Penrhyn Point (*Trwyn y Penrhyn*, Grid Ref. SH 629 796) for a spot of extra birding. Where the lane bends sharply beside a muddy and sandy bay, a short stretch of the old road makes a good place to park if you wish to take a look for any birds around. The rocks on the shore that are exposed at low tide make a good resting place for gulls, terns and cormorants, and if you check the rocky beach carefully, you are likely to see Oystercatchers, Turnstones and maybe Rock Pipits pottering about amongst the stones. If you cross over the road, take a look at the small pool and the surrounding field here where you may see Canada and Greylag Geese, Grey Herons, Redshanks, Curlews and other waders. This little corner has also provided a brief stopover for such rarities as Red-backed Shrike.

What other sights are nearby
- Historic town and castle in Beaumaris.
- Menai Bridge and Church Island.

- University town of Bangor.
- Anglesey Coastal Path.

Originally published in
Birds, Boots and Butties – Anglesey

by Ruth Miller

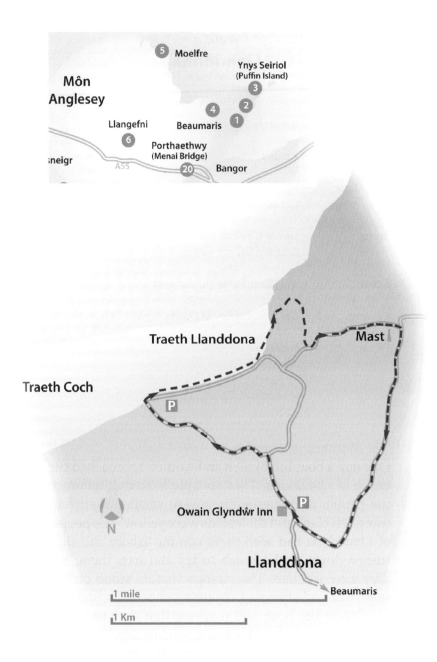

Walk 4
Llanddona

Walk details
Approx distance: *6 miles/9.6 kilometres*

Approx time:	*2 hours*
O.S. Maps:	*1:50 000 Landranger Sheet 114* *1:25 000 Explorer Sheet 263*
Start:	*Owain Glyndŵr Inn* *Grid Ref. SH 575 795*
Access:	*A545 Beaumaris – Llanddona.*
Parking:	*Car park in front of Owain Glyndŵr Inn.*
Please note:	*Mainly coastal path above the seashore. Sand-dunes can be muddy after heavy rain.*
Going:	*Moderate, cliff paths, lanes and beaches.*

The Witches of Llanddona – the legend
One day, a boat full of men and women approached the beach at Llanddona. These people looked different to the people of Anglesey, they were smaller, their hair was pitch black and their skins were yellow. The people of Llanddona had seen them coming ashore and they rushed down to the beach to try and stop them, but they were too late. The strange visitors stood on the sand, wet and shivering. There were no sails, steering or oars on the boat, and it seems that they had been sent from somewhere for being witches. They has been at sea for a long time and they were hungry and thirsty.

Looking down towards Traeth Coch from Llanddona

The people of Llanddona stood in a circle around them, watching them. The strange people asked for water, but no one offered any. Suddenly, one of them struck the sand with a stick and a fountain of clear water appeared.

Everyone was frightened; who were these strange people who could do such tricks? They then let the strange people leave the beach and they walked up the hill towards Llanddona. When they arrived there, they started building rough houses of stones and branches. Once they had settled in, the men started smuggling goods to earn a living whilst the women would walk around the area begging for food and money. Everyone was afraid of them and no one refused to give them what they wanted.

When the witches went to the local market to buy a pig, no one would bid against them in case they were cursed.

Everyone in the village were afraid of them. Some

said that they turned themselves into hares to make mischief. One day, a local man decided to try and get rid of one of them who had been a nuisance to him. He knew that an ordinary bullet would not kill a witch, therefore he put a piece of silver in his gun. He hit the witch and after that he had no trouble from him.

Another local man who was not afraid of them was Goronwy Tudur, but he had made every effort to keep them away from his house. Goronwy had grown a plant in front of his house which he knew the witches hated, and he had nailed a lucky horseshoe on every door that he had. He had also spread soil from the cemetery in every room, which was supposed to keep evil spirits away.

But one day he saw his cattle sitting in the field on their hind legs like cats. He knew that the witches had been there and had cursed the animals. Immediately, he burnt the skin of a snake and threw the ashes over the cows and they all, one by one, got up on four legs.

Another time, Goronwy was having difficulty making butter. He put the poker in the fire until it was red hot and then put it in the milk in the churn. Suddenly, a hare jumped out of the churn and ran away into the fields. It was one of the witches in disguise!

The most famous of the witches of Llanddona was Siân Bwt. Siân was very small, no more than about 110 centimetres high, so they say, and she had two thumbs on her left hand. Many say that the descendants of the witches still live in the village of Llanddona.

The walk
From Llanddona down to the beach and back into the village past the television mast.

Park your car near the Owain Glyndŵr Inn. For

those of you coming by bus, there is a bus stop before reaching the inn. In front of you, you will see a sign 'To the Beach'. Follow the road down hill towards the beach. When you come to the junction, turn left and then go down a steep hill towards the sea. At the bottom of the hill, follow the road to the right to a small car park and Caban y Traeth where you can buy something to eat or drink on the beach during summer.

To your left you will see a path going through the dunes. Follow it and you will reach the sands of Traeth Llanddona. To your left is Traeth Coch or Red Wharf Bay. Here, centuries ago, there was a bitter battle between the Welsh and the Vikings who had just landed on Anglesey. So many were killed in the battle, that the beach was red with blood, and it was called *traeth coch* or red beach after that.

Turn right and walk along the beach to the far end where you will see a Coastal Path sign. Follow the path up the steps to a kissing gate. Go through the gate and along the side of the field, and then follow the path up the slope towards a bungalow. Go over the stile and through the gate near a cottage, and then up the road past some houses.

At the junction, turn left and go up the steep hill towards the television mast. From here you will have a magnificent view of Traeth Coch and Traeth Llanddona. Continue along the road to the mast and the junction. Turn right and walk along the right-hand side of the road, facing the traffic. At the next junction,

The Menai Strait from Llanddona

turn right and go back towards Llanddona. Go past the housing estate on the right and back to the Owain Glyndŵr Inn.

Originally published in
Walking Adventures on Anglesey

by Dafydd Meirion

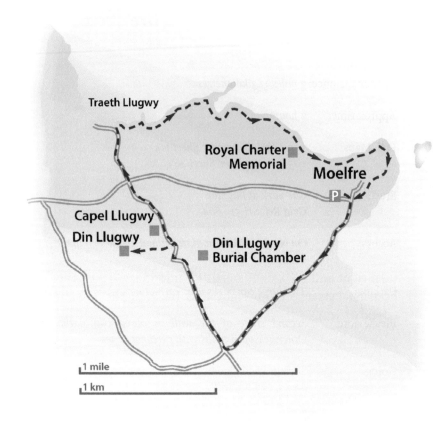

Traeth Llugwy

Royal Charter
Memorial

Moelfre

P

Capel Llugwy

Din Llugwy

Din Llugwy
Burial Chamber

1 mile

1 km

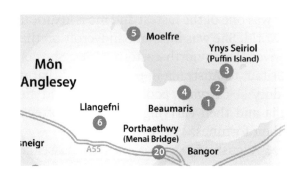

5 Moelfre

Ynys Seiriol
(Puffin Island)

Môn
Anglesey

3

4

2

Llangefni

Beaumaris

1

6

Porthaethwy
(Menai Bridge)

neigr

A55

20

Bangor

Walk 5
Royal Charter, Moelfre

Walk details
Approx distance: *7 miles/11.3 kilometres*

Approx time:	*2 hours*
O.S. Maps:	*1:50 000 Landranger Sheet 114* *1:25 000 Explorer Sheet 263*
Start:	*Car park at bus stop* *Grid Ref. SH 513 864*
Access:	*On reaching Moelfre, turn left and follow sign to the car park.*
Parking:	*Two large car parks near each other.*
Please note:	*Second stage of the walk is along cliff paths. Otherwise open paths with excellent views.*
Going:	*Tarmac road / quiet.* *Lanes, cliff top walks and fields.*

The *Royal Charter*
During the middle of the 19th century, the *Royal Charter* was one of the fastest and most luxurious ships in the world. She was built at Sandycroft on the banks of the river Dee in north-eastern Wales. She could sail from Britain to Australia in 60 days. And that was her main duty – carrying people to the gold fields of Australia and then carrying them back, often having made their fortunes.

On 26 August, 1859, there were 390 passengers and

A painting of the Royal Charter *at Oriel Môn*

numerous small boxes full of gold (worth £322,440) on board when the *Royal Charter* left Melbourne for Britain. Many of the passengers also carried money belts around their waists full of gold pieces. They had fine weather on the journey, and when the ship reached Ireland, the captain promised them that he would again have made the journey within 60 days.

But when they approached the coast of Anglesey, the wind strengthened and the weather got worse. But, rather than looking for shelter, the captain decided to hurry towards Liverpool as he had promised the passengers.

By six o'clock on 25 October, the *Royal Charter* had just gone past the Skerries, when the wind strengthened even more and began blowing the ship towards the shore. The captain fired a distress rocket to try and summon help, but the weather was too bad for any other ship to try and come to the rescue. The captain then lowered three anchors, but – one by one –

Llanallgo church

the heavy, thick cables broke, such was the strength of the wind blowing the ship towards the shore.

The passengers – men, women and children – were very frightened, and the captain came on deck to reassure them and to tell them that the ship was near the shore and that they would be rescued in the morning. And when dawn broke, everyone saw that they were only 23 metres from the shore. But there were huge waves between them and land, some as high as 20 metres.

One brave sailor offered to swim to the shore with a rope around his waist to take it to the people that had gathered on the beach to try and help the passengers. The sailor reached the beach and a small chair was tied to the rope. People were put one by one on the chair and pulled to safety.

But at seven o'clock, there was a huge bang and the *Royal Charter* broke in half. The passengers and crew were thrown into the foaming sea and some were crushed by the broken timbers of the ship. The sea was too stormy for anyone to try to rescue the people in the water.

Of the 490 people, including the crew, only 38 managed to reach the shore safely, and none of the children or women were rescued. Four hundred and sixty two people lost their lives, and their bodies were kept in Llanallgo church until they were buried in the cemetery. People from all over Britain came to Anglesey to see if their relatives were among the dead. Many reporters, also, came to the area to write stories for the newspapers about the awful tragedy, and amongst them was the famous author Charles Dickens.

About £300,000 worth of gold from the ship was found, but the authorities failed to find the rest. There were stories in the area that the locals had found some of the gold and hidden it in their cottages. And sometime during the last century, whilst renovating a house in the area, a bag with gold pieces in it was found hidden in the chimney.

A memorial to those who lost their lives was raised on the top of the cliff that looks out over the sea where one of the worst disasters at sea in Britain happened.

The walk
From Moelfre past the remains of the ancient village of Din Llugwy to the beach at Traeth Llugwy, past the *Royal Charter* Memorial and back to Moelfre.

If you arrive by car, leave it in the car park on the way into Moelfre to the right of the bus stop, where you will also arrive if coming by bus.

Walk out of the car park, and turn in the direction of the bus stop and walk to the crossroads. Turn right and go up the hill to a roundabout. Follow the signs to

The Brythonic village of Din Llugwy

Din Llugwy and Traeth Llugwy on your right.

Walk carefully along the road and you will reach Din Llugwy Burial Chamber. Why not have a look around?

Then, return to the road, and continue along it until you see the sign to Din Llugwy on your left. This village dates back to before

The magnificent ancient burial chamber of Din Llugwy, well worth a visit!

the Roman period and is worth visiting. On the way back you will see, to your left, an old church. This is Capel Llugwy; you can make a detour to visit it.

Go back to the road and turn left and walk in the same direction as you were before visiting Din Llugwy. At the crossroads, look carefully in both directions, and then go straight ahead, down the hill to the car park and beach at Traeth Llugwy.

There is a shop in the car park during the summer selling drinks and ice cream. You now have a choice: you can either walk back to Moelfre along the cliff top path that starts by the shop or go down to the beach and walk to the right until you reach the end and then go up the steps to the top of the cliff.

Whatever your decision, you will then be walking along the cliff top path. Before you reach the caravan park on the right, you will see the *Royal Charter* Memorial on a small hill with iron railings around it. Go past it until you see a stone stile; go over the stile and visit the Memorial.

The all-important Royal Charter *Memorial. A very important part of the village.*

Then, go back to the cliff top path and emerge into the caravan park. Go straight ahead, back on the cliff top walk.

Go through two large stones and turn right through two fields, until you come to a kissing gate. Then turn left and go down hill, passing a 'Private' sign, towards Moelfre Lifeboat House. It is possible, at certain times, to visit the lifeboat house.

Then go to the left, past the Moelfre Lifeboat Shop where you can find

The Dick Evans memorial at the Moelfre Lifeboat Centre.

Moelfre

information on the area and the surrounding sea. Why not call in and have a look? Continue down to the beach at Moelfre. Near the small car park is a shop where they sell drinks and snacks.

After passing the shop, go up the hill to the crossroads, and turn left either to the bus stop or the car park where you started the walk.

Originally published in
Walking Adventures on Anglesey

by Dafydd Meirion

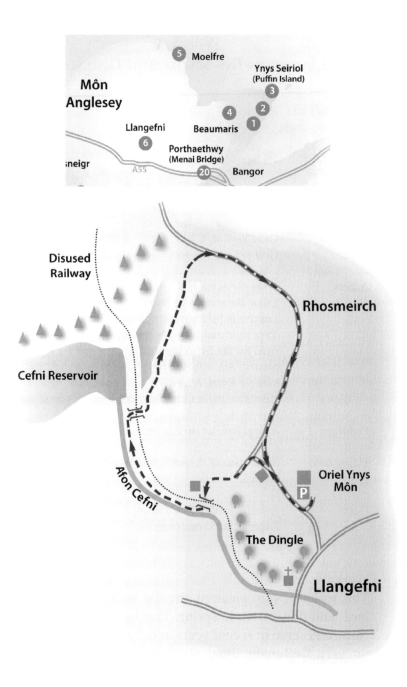

Walk 6
Llangefni Reservoir and Dingle

Walk details
Approx distance: *5 miles/8 kilometres*

Approx time: *2½ hours*

O.S. Maps: *1:50 000 Landranger Sheet 114*
1:25 000 Explorer Sheet 263

Start: *Oriel Ynys Môn*
Grid Ref. SH 459 766

Access: *From the A55 take the A5114 exit for Llangefni and follow the main road into the town centre. At a T-junction in the town centre, turn left onto the B5420. Turn right and follow the one-way system, following signs for the B5110 towards Benllech and the B5111 towards Amlwch. At a fork, turn left up a slight hill onto the B5111. After a left-hand bend, turn right at a brown sign for Oriel Ynys Môn and golf course.*

Parking: *A large free car park at Oriel Ynys Môn.*

Please note: *Some areas of the path could flood after very heavy rainfall.*

Going: *Lakeside / valley floor / busy.*
Lakeside, paths and lanes.

Walk description
This makes a very pleasant circular walk, particularly bird- and flower-rich in spring. Thanks to work on the Nature Reserve in recent years, much of the walking is on very well-maintained slate paths or boardwalks

The Dingle

which lead you close to, and even in one place right on top of, the fast-flowing water of Afon Cefni! Meandering through the secluded woodland of The Dingle is particularly enjoyable in spring when it is full of bird song all around you and wild flowers at your feet. This makes a great contrast to the open space of the Cefni Reservoir with its population of wildfowl and gulls.

Walk directions
Check the car park before heading off on your walk. You are very likely to see Pied Wagtails strutting around the car park itself while the surrounding tall trees are a good place for the more common woodland

birds such as Great Tit, Blue Tit, Chaffinch and Robin. Ravens can occur at any time on this walk, wheeling overhead; listen out for their distinctive 'kronk' call which can carry a long way. Other birds such as Woodpigeon, Magpies, Carrion Crows and Jackdaws are also likely here.

Leaving the car park at Oriel Ynys Môn, continue uphill along the main road for a short distance. Take care along this stretch; there is a pavement but the traffic tends to travel quite fast along here. After ¼ mile/0.4 km, fork left onto a narrow lane called Pencoed. At the T-junction, turn left.

Check this stretch for hedgerow birds such as Dunnock and Wren. Fence posts and telegraph poles make good lookout posts for Buzzards, while Mistle Thrushes may be seen probing the grassy fields for food.

After a short distance you will reach a fork in the road. Continue straight ahead here, ignoring a track and cattle grid off to your right. Go through the footpath gate and follow the tarmac track as it descends down and right into the valley of Afon Cefni. Continue past the white cottage on your right until you reach the footpath in the valley and turn right. This is also a cycle path so it may become busier at peak times in the holiday season and at weekends. Go through the gate and under the old railway bridge.

The historical railway bridge – a reminder of the area's past

*Continue along the footpath with the disused railway on
your right and Afon Cefni on your left.*

This stretch of river used to be a good spot for Dipper,
so keep your eyes peeled for this dapper brown bird
with a white bib as it bobs up and down on small rocks
in the river, in case one reappears. You are very likely
to see a Grey Wagtail on this clear fast-flowing water too.

*Ignore a footpath off to your left and continue along the
slate track.*

The area of scrubby bush and willows along the
disused railway is a likely area in spring for migrants
such as Common Whitethroats, Chiffchaffs, Willow
Warblers and Blackcaps, so it is well worth checking
this spot thoroughly. Keep an eye out at any time of
year for Reed Buntings in the reeds to the left of the
path, and you may also see Treecreepers working their
way up the trunks of the trees here.

*The path now crosses the river on a wooden bridge which
then becomes a raised boardwalk. The path is cantilevered
so it overhangs the river itself as the boardwalk clings to the
side of the cliff, quite a feat of carpentry.*

This is another good stretch to look for Dipper, while
the reed beds on either side of the rusty railway tracks
are a good place to look and listen for Reed and Sedge
Warblers in spring. To be sure of your Reed Warbler,
look out for its plain brown face lacking an obvious eye
stripe and listen for its rather monotonous song which
chugs along with very little variation in pitch. The
Sedge Warbler on the other hand has a broad white eye

stripe and has a more scratchy erratic song with much more variation in pitch.

Back on terra firma again, the now-concrete path crosses an area of floodplain, and the sign warns that the path itself is liable to flood!

This reedy area is another good spot for Sedge Warblers in spring, and may well conceal well-camouflaged Common Snipe too.

Continue through the wooden gate. You are now approaching Llyn Cefni reservoir and because of the land levels here, you will experience the rather odd sensation of being at eye-level with the water itself.

The Llangefni reservoir, where you may experience the sensation of being eye-level with the water

The area below the weir is covered in low scrub, ideal habitat for Cetti's Warblers, whose explosive calls may burst from well within the bush as the bird itself skulks out of sight. Check the stream below the weir for Grey Wagtails.

Ignore the footpath heading off to the left, and continue walking towards the reservoir. As the slate path bends sharply to the right to zigzag up to the footbridge over the railway, leave the path here and climb up the grassy bank to the edge of the reservoir itself.

This is an excellent place to scan the open water. Coots are common here, and duck species should include

Mallard and Tufted Duck all year, while winter visitors are likely to include Wigeon and Goldeneye. Canada and Greylag Geese can be found here all year, though the flocks may be larger in winter. This is a good place to look for gulls too: Black-headed and Common Gulls should be here all year, while Lesser Black-backed Gulls are possible from spring through to September. Look out for Great Crested Grebes displaying in spring and they should still be here in summer, while Little Grebes can be heard, if not seen, all year round.

By now the footpath beside the reservoir is overgrown, and where the map indicates to cross the railway line, there is a sign which says: 'Anyone caught tresspassing on the railway line will be fined £1,000'.

So, I recommend this route:

After viewing the reservoir, retrace your steps back to the path and bear left up the zigzag path over the wooden bridge that crosses over the disused railway line.

Continue along this path for about 1 mile/1.6 kilometres through the pine forest. If you look to your left you will see the reservoir through the trees.

At the end of this path you will emerge onto the main road. Turn right here and walk along the pavement.

Continue through the village of Rhosmeirch, until after a good distance since leaving the pine forest you will reach Oriel Ynys Môn and the car park on your left.

What to look for ...

... in spring/summer: Look out for the arrival of spring migrants particularly in the areas of willow, where you may encounter Willow Warblers, Chiffchaffs, Common Whitethroats, Blackcaps, Garden Warblers. In the reedy areas, listen out for Sedge and Reed

Warblers calling, while Cetti's Warbler song may burst out of the scrubby bushes below the weir. Lesser Black-backed Gulls may start appearing out on the open water of the reservoir at this time of year, as well as Great Crested Grebes: look out for them performing their stunning mating dance. Swifts, Swallows, Sand and House Martins are likely to be hawking over the water for insects as spring progresses into summer. Ospreys have been seen on their northerly migration but you would be very lucky to see one!

... in autumn: Wildfowl numbers out on the reservoir start to build up with the arrival of Pochard, Gadwall, Shoveler, Teal, Goldeneye and Wigeon; the shallow east end is the best area. There have also been occasional records of Garganey here in August and September. Check the flocks of Teal carefully, as Garganey will sometimes associate with them.

... in winter: Check the fields at the start of your walk for Fieldfares and Redwings looking for food amongst the grass. You should still be able to see the autumn duck arrivals at this time of year, and bird numbers on the reservoir will also be boosted by gull species such as Black-headed and Common Gulls. Check the flocks carefully for scarcer species. Mediterranean Gulls have occurred here on a number of occasions and a Glaucous Gull on rare occasions. If you are very lucky, you may flush a Woodcock from the damp wooded area on the far side of the reservoir, while similarly, Common Snipe may lurk in the reeds and rough grasses of the water meadows beside the disused railway. A small flock of Whooper Swans winters on fields north of the reservoir and occasionally visits the water. Early mornings can be the best time to see them. Peregrine Falcons hunt the area but tend to move through very quickly, so you will have to be alert to see one.

... all year round: Resident hedgerow birds such as Dunnock, Wren, Robin, Blackbird, Song and Mistle Thrushes should put in an appearance along the peaceful lanes at the start of your walk. You are likely to see Reed Buntings in the reedbeds beside the disused railway line at any time of year. You should see some species of wildfowl at any time of year out on the reservoir, such as Mallard, Tufted Duck, Greylag and Canada Geese, Mute Swan, while Little Grebe, Moorhen and Coot will also be there. In the woodland areas, you should be able to find Goldcrests, as well as Coal, Great, Blue and Long-tailed Tits at any time of year, while Great Spotted Woodpeckers, Nuthatches, and Jays make themselves heard if not always seen. Sharp eyes may pick out a Treecreeper working its way up the treetrunk. Buzzards and Ravens are easy to see and you may also see the occasional Kestrel or Sparrowhawk. If you are lucky, you may also encounter Crossbills and Lesser Redpolls in any larch trees; around the car park is a particularly good spot.

Male Reed Bunting

Where to eat

Within the same building as the Oriel Ynys Môn is the popular licensed café Blas Mwy, which is open seven days a week from 10.30 a.m. to 5 p.m. It offers hot and cold drinks, homemade snacks, cakes and light meals.

Other information

- Free parking at Oriel Ynys Môn.
- Toilets and gift shop in the art gallery building.

What other sights are nearby

- Malltraeth RSPB Reserve.
- The historic suspension bridge and town of Menai Bridge.
- Church Island and views of the Menai Strait.

Originally published in
Birds, Boots and Butties – Anglesey

by Ruth Miller

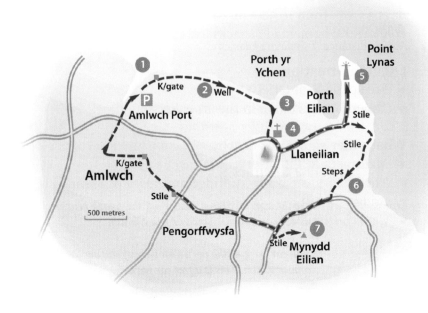

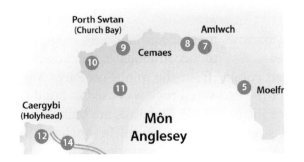

Walk 7
Porth Amlwch

Walk details
Approx distance: *7½ miles/12 kilometres*

Approx time: *3 hours*

O.S. Maps: *1:50 000 Landranger Sheet 114*
                 1:25 000 Explorer Sheet 263

Start: *Porth Amlwch*
                 Grid Ref. SH 453937

Access: *Take the sign for 'Town Centre' off the A5025 near Amlwch, and follow signs to Porth Amlwch.*

Parking: *Small car park at the port. Can be busy during the summer season. This is a free car park.*

Please note: *Fields can be wet after heavy rainfall. High cliff near the well (Point 2 on the map).*

Going: *Cliff side and quiet lanes.*

Points of Interest
1. The narrow, natural harbour was enlarged about 200 years ago to accommodate the vessels which exported copper from the mines on Parys Mountain. Some of the excavated rock was used to build the pier and face the dock wall. The walls are built of vertically placed stone which is unusual in Anglesey and the method may have been introduced to Amlwch by Cornishmen seeking work in the copper mines.

Parys Mountain copper mines

2. The remains of a square, walled enclosure is just visible under a large rock, a short distance from the stream. This is the site of Ffynnon Eilian, the well of St Eilian. For many centuries it was believed that the well water could cure various ailments. Drinking the water was followed by rituals of prayer at the well and offerings placed in the church. More recently, the well has been used as a cursing well. One practice was to scratch the cursed person's initials on a piece of slate and place it in the well.

3. Eilian is said to have landed at Porth yr Ychen in the 6th century. He came from Rome with his family and cattle and built a church nearby. Eilian had to excommunicate and blind Caswallon Law Hir (*Caswallon the Long Handed*) who had commited a misdemeanour. However, Caswallon was forgiven, his sight restored, and in return, Eilian was given land to build his church. He could have all the land crossed by

his hart before it was caught by Caswallon's hounds. Starting at Dulas, the chase went to Parys Mountain and finished at Llam y Carw (*Hart's Leap*) where the deer escaped the dogs by jumping across the gorge. The land St Eilian was given for his church comprised this corner of Anglesey bounded by Dulas, Parys Mountain and Amlwch to Point Lynas.

St Eilian's church

4. The oldest part of St Eilian's church is the 12th century tower which has a pyramid shaped roof. Most of the remainder of the church was rebuilt in the 15th century. A short 17th century passage joins the chancel to the small chapel of St Eilian. On the rood-screen there is a lugubrious painting of a skeleton.

5. In the 18th century the Mersey pilots had a watch-house here with a light consisting of a candle with two reflectors. It was replaced in 1835 by the present lighthouse which now has an automatic beacon. This is a good site to watch birds on migration – in late summer gannets, skuas and manx shearwaters fly past the headland. Sometimes there is a glimpse of a dolphin or porpoise.

6. The white building above here was once a semaphore station, one of a chain between Holyhead and Liverpool. During the 18th and 19th centuries ship

owners and merchants were in need of some kind of news system to let them know their ships and cargo were approaching Liverpool. The first signal was on Bidston Hill for ships entering the river Mersey. The system was extended and in 1827 communication by semaphore was established between Liverpool and Holyhead. The apparatus consisted of a visual code on moveable arms.

7. From Mynydd Eilian there are fine views of northern Anglesey, Holyhead Mountain and the mainland. On very clear days it may be possible to see the mountains of the Lake District and southern Ireland. Much closer is the scarred hill of Parys Mountain, where copper extraction began in the Bronze Age. Recent excavation has uncovered primitive stone hammers dating 2000-1500 BC. Ingots of copper with Roman inscriptions have been found on the side of the mountain. The greatest activity came in the 18th century when two mines, the Parys Mine and the Mona Mine, were operating on the mountain and exporting all over the world. Copper was used to make nails and bolts and to sheathe the hulls of wooden ships to reduce damage by marine organisms. Amlwch's harbour was enlarged and the town's population swelled to 6,000. The conspicious windmill on the mountain's summit was built in 1878 to assist in pumping water, a source of copper. Water was pumped from the workings into ponds containing scrap iron. Chemical reaction between the copper solution and iron caused the copper to precipitate out resulting in a sludge of copper, which was dried and smelted. The water, without its copper but rich in iron, was channelled into pools and it deposited yellow ochre,

Porth Amlwch

used in paint. These precipitation pits and ochre pools can be seen on the east and south sides of Parys Mountain.

Walk directions   (-) **denotes Point of Interest**
From the car park above Amlwch harbour (1) walk towards a house and go through a kissing gate on the right.

Follow the narrow path along the coast to a ladder stile and cross a stream (2). Continue on the coast path and after passing through a small gate cross a stile at Porth yr Ychen (3).

Don't cross the stile ahead. Bear right to follow the right edge of the field uphill to a track. Go through a gate and farmyard. Take the left-hand of two gates. Cross steps to reach the lane and Llaneilian church (4).

The lighthouse at Point Lynas

Turn left at the church and left again. Walk downhill to the slipway at Porth Eilian.

Bear right and follow the road the Point Lynas lighthouse (5).

Return along the road to some gateposts. In about another 100 metres turn left to a stile.

Follow the wall on the right and at a corner keep ahead to the coast. Bear right, with the sea on the left, and at the next fence ignore the stile nearest the sea but go uphill to the ladder stile.

Continue uphill to a kissing gate. Bear right and follow the right boundary to the next kissing gate. Go half-left to a marker post below a gorse bush and continue to a ladder stile.

The path bears right through gorse. Reach a marker post and continue to a wall (6). Bear right to an enclosed track. Pass a barn and reach a stile.

Cross a track and go up steps. Take a path to the corner of a high wall. Continue with the wall on the left to a kissing gate. Bear right to cross a field and keep ahead to a building and walled path. Join a track and follow it uphill to a lane.

Point Lynas

Turn right on the lane. Where the lane bends right go left on a narrow road. In a few paces bear left to a stile. Follow the path to the trig point on Mynydd Eilian (7).

Return to the narrow road and lane. Turn left downhill to Pengorffwysfa. Bear right and immediately left in the direction of Amlwch.

At the next road junction turn right and in a few paces go left on a track. Pass to the right of a house to reach a ladder stile.

Follow an enclosed path to a field. Bear right between rock outcrops and aim for the roof of a house seen in trees ahead. Go through a wall gap and follow a wall on the left. Reach another wall and bear left to follow the wall on the right to a stile.

The bay at Point Lynas

Turn right to reach a track coming from the house. Keep ahead and when the track bends right, turn left to a kissing gate.

Follow the left fence. At the field corner ignore a kissing gate on the left but go through the one ahead.

After passing through gorse bear left to follow a wall on the left. Cross a broken low gate and stream to reach a path junction.

Turn right on a clear path. Ignore a path on the right and turn left to a kissing gate at houses.

Keep ahead to a road. Turn left then right to pass the Adelphi.

Fork left to the slipway. Take a path on the right and

continue along the harbour. Bear right up steps and walk past the old Shell buildings to the car park.

Facilities
Full facilities in Amlwch. Toilets near Porth Eilian. Camping at Llaneilian.

Originally published in
Circular Walks on Anglesey

by Dorothy Hamilton

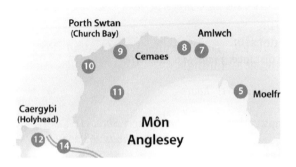

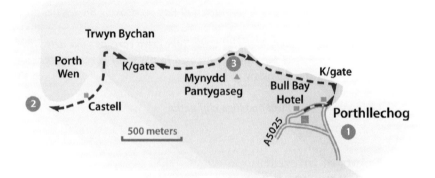

Walk 8
Porthllechog/Bull Bay

Walk details
Approx distance: *3 miles/4.8 kilometres*

Approx time:	*1½ hours*
O.S. Maps:	*1:50 000 Landranger Sheet 114*
	1:25 000 Explorer Sheets 262/263
Start:	*Bull Bay Harbour*
	Grid Ref. SH 426 944
Access:	*2 miles west of Amlwch on the A5025 you come into Bull Bay. Park on the right by the harbour. Buses from Amlwch and Holyhead.*
Parking:	*Small parking by the harbour. Alternatively you can park by the main road in a large parking on your right as you enter Bull Bay overlooking the sea.*
Please note:	*Very high cliff walk. Take extra care, as some areas of the path are exposed to the many coves and the sea below.*
Going:	*Field and high cliff paths.*

Points of Interest
1. Bull Bay (*Porthllechog*) was once a busy little fishing port and ships were built here in the 19th century. It also had a pilot station with two four-oared boats. Steamers from Liverpool used to call at the northern end of the bay to land passengers and stores.

Porth Llechog

2. The abandoned Porth Wen brickworks is situated in a spectacular position on the west side of the bay. It closed about the time of the First World War. Quartzite from a quarry on Craig Wen, the hill behind, was send down an incline to the brickworks where it was made into silica bricks, which were used in the steel industry. They were exported by boat from the quay. The tall chimneys and beehive shaped kilns survive alongside the shell of the brickworks.

3. The small island called East Mouse (*Ynys Amlwch*) is visible ahead on the eastern side of Bull Bay. Between the island and the chemical works lies the wreck of the *Dakota*, a huge steamship which had been making the transatlantic crossing from Liverpool to New York in May 1877. The ship, built for speed, was steaming at 14 knots about two miles offshore when the course was changed. The ship should have gone further from land

but for some unfathomable reason she headed towards the coast and hit rocks. Bull Bay lifeboat rescued the passengers. Another wreck, close to Bull Bay but near the western side, is *HMS Pansy*. This Wallasey paddle steamer, taken over by the Admirality, sank in a north-easterly gale in 1916.

Starting point of the walk, with the magnificent view of the Irish Sea

Walk directions (-) **denotes Point of Interest**
Leave the harbour (1) by taking the lane opposite. Pass the car park and picnic tables. Take a footpath at the bottom of the hill. Emerge onto road and turn right.

Go left downhill on a narrow path through bushes. It rises to a kissing gate.

This is a reminder of the dangerous high-cliff path of Bull Bay

   The first section of the walk has been closed up and changed over the years, so according to local people, they suggest visiting Porth Wen along the coastal path, and returning back along the same route.

Turn right here and follow the field to a second kissing gate.

Porth Wen's industrial remains

One of the many kissing gates of Bull Bay

Go through a further two kissing gates.

You have now a superb view of Porth Wen and its brickworks chimney in the distance.

Continue as far as you desire, then turn back and return to the car park along the same coastal path you came on.

Facilities

Toilets and picnic tables near the car park. The Bull Bay Hotel, near the start/end of the walk, is open to non-residents.

The beautiful small port at Bull Bay, with its many small boats

Originally published in
Circular Walks on Anglesey

by Dorothy Hamilton

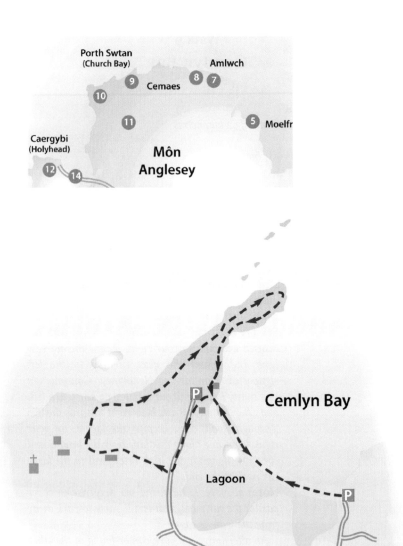

Walk 9
Cemlyn Bay

Walk details

Approx distance: *2 miles/3.2 kilometres*

Approx time: *1½ hours*

O.S. Maps: *1:50 000 Landranger Sheet 114*
1:25 000 Explorer Sheet 262

Start: *Cemlyn Bay car park*
Grid Ref. SH 329 936

Access: *Head north on the A5025 towards Cemaes. Turn left onto a narrow minor road at Caerdegog Uchaf, where the A road bends to the right (Grid Ref. SH 343 913) and immediately left again with the disused windmill to your right. Follow this narrow lane and ignore the next turning to the left signposted Llanfair-yng-Nghornwy. Continue on this twisty lane for about 2 miles/3.2 km. Turn left, and after ½ mile/0.8 km, bear right towards the 'No Through Road' sign, keeping the lagoon on your right. Continue along this lane over the bridge, and continue alongside the high brick wall to the large car park at the end.*
Note: *at extreme tides, the sea may rise to cover part of the car park, so it is advisable to park away from the water's edge.*

An alternative car park can be found at the other end of the shingle ridge (Grid Ref. SH 337 932). To reach this, follow the same route as above. After following the twisty lane for 2 miles/3.2 km, do not turn left but continue round to the right and take the left fork to the car park at the next junction.

Parking: *A large stony car park.*

Please note:	*Fields may be wet/muddy after heavy rainfall.*
	Poor sea defence in the car park.
Going:	*Quiet / muddy.*
	Fields and coastal paths mainly.

Site highlights

- Close views of one of Britain's largest tern colonies in breeding season.
- High occurrence of rare and unusual species.
- Variety of habitat including saltwater lagoon, shoreline, pasture and scrubland.
- Easy walking in stunning coastal scenery.

Walk description

'Expect the unexpected' must be the watchword for this birding Mecca on the Welsh mainland. Only the island of Bardsey, Llŷn can beat Cemlyn for attracting good birds and rarities throughout the year. The list of stunning unusual and rare birds to pop up here over the years is long and illustrious, and includes such far-flung travellers as American Golden Plover, Lesser Yellowlegs, Black-winged Stilts, Cayenne Tern, Sooty Tern, Bridled Tern, Black-headed Bunting, Woodchat Shrike and Blue-winged Teal, to name but some. Visit here in the breeding season, and even if there are no rarities about, you will still enjoy stunning close-up views of the amazing tern colony on the lagoon. The variety of habitat, including saltwater lagoon, rough pasture, rocky shoreline and scrubby bush ensures a range of waders, wildfowl, shorebirds and passerines are there for you to discover at any time of year. Add the possibility of seeing seals and dolphins from this

Cemlyn Bay

stunning coastline, and you can appreciate the appeal of this wonderful place and want to return here again and again.

Walk directions

Firstly, if the tide permits, it is well worth walking out onto the shingle ridge to view the bay and island on the lagoon. From the car park, follow the footpath sign. Cross the outlet stream by the concrete causeway and make your way out onto the shingle ridge. Note: at high tide, these rocks are covered and the stream flows surprisingly fast over the causeway. You can still wade across but the water may be deeper and colder than you expect. I speak from experience!

This shingle ridge, or *esgair*, has been formed by the action of the waves and wind depositing rocks and shingle across the bay to create a lagoon trapped behind it. This lagoon is fed by a freshwater stream, with an input of saltwater at high tides only. The

Another view of the bay

protected brackish water that results is a haven for waders and wildfowl, and the site is managed as a nature reserve by the North Wales Wildlife Trust on lease from the National Trust, which owns much of this coastline. This spot regularly attracts unusual species: the regulars such as Red-breasted Mergansers, Shelducks, Redshanks, Oystercatchers and Ringed Plovers have in the past been joined by more scarce species such as Garganey, Red-necked Phalarope, American Golden Plover, Terek Sandpiper, and Blue-winged Teal.

The island on the lagoon holds one of Britain's largest tern colonies during the spring breeding season. Excellent views can be had of the Sandwich, Common and Arctic Terns from the shingle ridge, though people are asked to keep to a restricted viewing area during certain months so as to minimise any disruption to the birds. The close views of these birds, either sitting on eggs or commuting continuously to and fro with fish, as well as the noise and smell from this bustling colony, will make a lasting impression upon you. Again, in addition to the more common species, this colony has over the years attracted such unusual visitors as Cayenne, Sooty, Bridled, Caspian and Whiskered Terns.

You cannot fail to notice Wylfa nuclear power station in the distance. It was the last and largest of its type to be built, and has been supplying electricity since 1971. It is scheduled to close down in 2010, at which point the fuel will be gradually removed and sent to Sellafield to be treated.

Retrace your steps back to the car park, and walk back down the lane, with the brick wall to your left until you reach the bridge.

Where you cross the bridge, take the time to scan back across the lagoon to view the other side of the tern island. It is also worth studying the narrow body of water on your right for any birds that may be quietly skulking in the edge of the reeds.

Turn right and walk along the farm lane beside the lake, checking the bushes, fields and water for birds. After a right-hand bend, just before you reach the farm, go through a field gate on your right and walk slightly uphill towards the coast, keeping to the left hand edge of the field.

These marshy fields can be rather muddy underfoot, but can also hold birds such as Yellow Wagtails, Meadow Pipits, Linnets, and have even provided a temporary resting spot for Black-winged Stilts, Pectoral Sandpiper, Lesser Yellowlegs, Tawny Pipits and Lapland Buntings. The marsh flowers, including Flag Iris, add a bold note of colour here in summer.

At the top of the field where you reach the cliff edge, you join the Anglesey Coastal Path. For this walk, turn right and continue through a series of kissing gates along the field edges, with the rocky shore on your left.

Check the shore for any birds down amongst the rocks, including Oystercatchers, Turnstones, Cormorants and gulls. If you are lucky, you may spot Grey Seals either resting full length on the small island just offshore or bobbing about in the water, casting a curious eye over any walkers nearby. Dolphins have also been seen offshore, more frequently Bottlenosed Dolphins, but pods of Risso's Dolphins have also been recorded.

A wooden bench looking out to sea provides a convenient resting place for scanning the sea and shore. From here, you can walk around the grassy headland for a view of the bay. Alternatively, take the footpath to your right which leads directly back to the car park.

You will pass a memorial commemorating the 150th anniversary of the first lifeboat commissioned on Anglesey (1828-1978). This service was founded by the Reverend James Williams and his wife Frances, after they witnessed the death of 145 people when the Irish Packetboat, The *Alert*, ran aground on West Mouse island in 1823.

Right up until the minute you drive off in your car, it is worth checking the shoreline and the bushes and fields around the car park. The scrubby bushes have in the

Common Tern

past provided cover for Common Rosefinch, Woodchat Shrike and Melodious Warbler, so you can almost expect the unexpected here.

What to look for ...
... in late spring/summer: You cannot miss the tern colony on the island in the lagoon. Look out for Common, Sandwich and Arctic Terns, while occasionally Roseate Terns still visit this site. Rare terns have also frequented the lagoon, including Cayenne, Sooty, Bridled, Caspian and Whiskered Terns. The island also attracts nesting Black-headed Gulls.

... in summer: As you walk across the fields, you should see and hear Skylarks singing on the wing, while Meadow Pipits and Linnets rise up at your feet. Check the damp field beside the narrow lane towards the farm for Yellow Wagtail.

... in autumn: Looking out to sea, you may catch sight of Fulmars, Manx Shearwaters and Gannets flying past. Along the shoreline, keep an eye open for Purple Sandpipers, Dunlins, Whimbrels, Common Sandpipers and Turnstones. Other waders such as Golden Plovers, Grey Plovers, Lapwings and Knots are also likely here. Snow Buntings may be seen, and Wheatears on passage too. And of course, this is Cemlyn, so scarce and rare migrants may also turn up.

... in winter: Red-breasted Mergansers, some Teal and Wigeon should be seen on the lagoon, and other duck such as Goldeneye and Gadwall may occur.

... all year round: At any time of year you should see Shelducks on the lagoon and Grey Herons fishing on its edges. Along the shoreline, look out for Redshanks, Oystercatchers, Cormorants and gulls, and look across to the little islands just offshore, and you're likely to see Grey Seals, either basking on the island or bobbing in the water here. Meadow Pipits and Stonechats should be easy to see on the grassland and fenceposts. Looking upwards, you should see Buzzards over the farmland, while Ravens and Choughs are more likely to be enjoying the thermals along the coastline.

Where to eat
'The Jam Factory' at the nearby hamlet of Nanner (Grid Ref. SH 335 920) makes jam and honey on the premises for sale, and also has a Coffee and Tea Shop offering hot and cold drinks, snacks and homemade cakes. Telephone: 01407 711 588.

Other information
- Free car park.
- No public toilets on site, the nearest are in Cemaes. Toilets at The Jam Factory for customers only.
- Causeway to shingle beach covered at high tide, and car park may be flooded by exceptional tides.
- The North Wales Wildlife Trusts viewing instructions to be followed to avoid disturbance during breeding season.

What other sights are nearby
- Anglesey Coastal Path in both directions.
- National Trust coastline at Carmel Head is a good birding area.
- Point Lynas with its lighthouse is an excellent spot for sea-watching.
- Wylfa Nuclear Power Station, visitor centre is open 10 a.m. to 4 p.m. daily, free entrance, café on-site.

Originally published in
Birds, Boots and Butties – Anglesey

by Ruth Miller

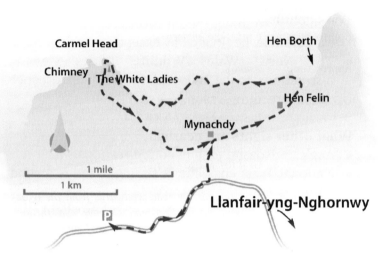

Carmel Head

Hen Borth

Chimney

The White Ladies

Hen Felin

Mynachdy

1 mile

1 km

Llanfair-yng-Nghornwy

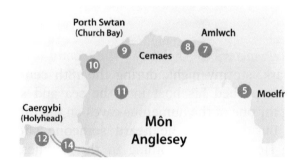

Porth Swtan
(Church Bay)

Amlwch

(9)

Cemaes

(8) (7)

(10)

(11)

(5) **Moelfr**

Caergybi
(Holyhead)

Môn
Anglesey

(12) (14)

Walk 10
The Bonesetters of Anglesey

Walk details
Approx distance: *6 miles/9.6 kilometres*

Approx time: *2 hours*

O.S. Maps: *1:50 000 Landranger Sheet 114*
                 1:25 000 Explorer Sheet 262

Start: *Mynachdy car park*
                 Grid Ref. SH 303 904

Access: *Take the narrow road westwards from the A5025*
                 between Llanfaethlu and Cemaes. Go through
                 Llanfair-yng-Nghornwy village, and about 1½ miles
                 outside the village there is a car park on your right-
                 hand side.

Parking: *Small stony National Trust car park.*

Please note: *Fields can be wet/muddy after heavy rainfall.*

Going: *Hillside / quiet.*
                 Fields, lanes, beaches and pleasant coastal paths.

The Bonesetters of Anglesey – the legend
One dark, stormy night, during the 18th century, a smuggler pushed his boat into the sea and started rowing for one of the numerous caves on the Anglesey coast. But suddenly, he heard someone shouting 'Help!' He could see nothing in the darkness, but started rowing towards the cries.

He then came across a small boat with two boys clutching tightly to it. The smuggler pulled the boys

Llanfair-yng-Nghornwy church

into his boat and started rowing furiously to the shore, but one of the boys had already died before he reached safety. About half a mile from the shore was Mynachdy where Dr Lloyd lived. The smuggler took the boy to him.

Slowly, the boy came round, but they could not find where he had come from because he could speak no Welsh or English. They learnt that he was called Evan or something similar, and in later years the local people though that he might have come from a Spanish ship which had sunk on the Skerries rocks.

Evan stayed with Dr Lloyd and he was given the surname Thomas. One day Dr Lloyd was about to kill one of his hens for Sunday dinner as it had broken one of its legs. But Evan got hold of the hen, set the bones and made a small splint to keep them in place until they mended.

After a while, Evan would accompany Dr Lloyd when he went to see his patients. At first, Evan would mend the broken bones of the patients' animals, but later he was allowed to set the bones of the patients themselves. The story of Evan's skills rapidly spread through Anglesey and people from all over the island came to see him to mend their bones.

And it wasn't only Evan Thomas who had this skill. Every one of his sons could also mend bones. If you go for a walk to Church Bay on the island, you will go past a house called Cilmaenan. There is a plaque on the side of the house saying that a son of Evan Thomas, Richard Evans (1772-1851), had lived there.

One of Evan Thomas's nephews, of the same name as him, opened a surgery in Liverpool and became a wealthy man. He had seven children and one of them, Hugh Owen Thomas, trained to become a doctor. He became famous throughout Britain as an orthopaedic (bone) surgeon, and he devised many things for the medical profession, including the Thomas splint to hold broken bones together.

His nephew, Sir Robert Jones, opened the famous orthopaedic hospital in Gobowen on the Welsh-English border which treats many people from north and mid Wales and the English Midlands.

Walk directions
From Mynachdy near Llanfair-yng-Nghornwy to Hen Borth and Carmel Head and back.

* In order that you don't disturb the wildlife, you can only do this walk between 1 February and 14 September.

Go off the A5025 and turn towards Llanfair-yng-Nghornwy. Go through and out of the village until you come to a crossroads. To the right is a sign saying Private Road. Continue up the left-hand bend and continue on the road for about ½ mile. You will come to a National Trust sign on your right and there is a car park here. (There is no bus service.)

The lane which leads down to Mynachdy Farm

Turn left out of the car park, and continue down to the post box. Turn left onto the Private Road, past a house on the right and continue to Mynachdy farm where Dr Lloyd lived. Go into the farmyard, and then through the gate on your right, following the track across the field to a gate and stone stile. Over the stile and along the field to a gate. Don't go through the gate but go to the wooden stile on the right.

Go over the stile and down the path to Hen Felin. Near the Hen Felin gate there is a footpath sign to your left. Go through the small gate and over the footbridge and through the kissing gate. Walk along the side of the field and you will arrive on the beach at Hen Borth. Turn left and walk between two fences to a gate and kissing gate. Go through the kissing gate and either walk on the beach or on the path above the beach until you come to another kissing gate.

Walk along the coastal path, often above a small cliff. Out in the sea, you will see West Mouse island and the Skerries where Evan Thomas was probably shipwrecked. To your right you will see a Danger sign warning you to keep away from an old mine shaft.

Continue along the path, over the stile, then over a footbridge and follow the path up the slope. Over another footbridge and over two stone stiles.

You will then see the White Ladies. These are white triangular towers – two on the mainland and one on West Mouse. They are in one long line and were used by sea captains to navigate around Carmel Head.

You will now have reached Carmel Head – about half way through the walk. Why not stop here for a picnic? In front of you, there is a tall chimney and if you go towards it you will find the remains of an old copper mine. Copper ore used to be burnt in the furnace under the chimney. It is said that copper was mined here thousands of years ago.

Walk now towards the White Lady furthest from the sea. Then turn left and walk towards a gap in the wall. Walk along the path towards a small forest. Keep to the right of the forest and follow the path between the trees and a rock until you come to a gate and stone stile.

Go over the stile and follow the path to a small lake (this may be dry in summer). Continue to a gate and stile and then down towards a larger lake. Follow the concrete track in front of the dam to another gate and stone stile. Over the stile and continue along the track to another gate and stone stile and back to Mynachdy farm.

Turn right and then walk back to the car.

Originally published in
Walking Adventures on Anglesey

by Dafydd Meirion

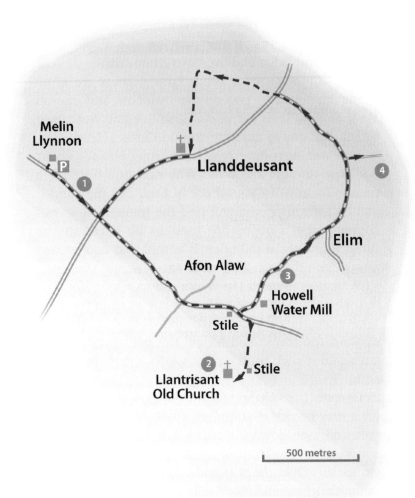

Melin
Llynnon

Llanddeusant

4

Elim

Afon Alaw

3

Howell
Water Mill

Stile

2

Stile

Llantrisant
Old Church

500 metres

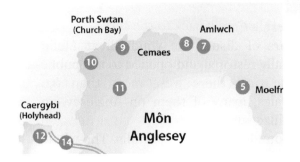

Porth Swtan
(Church Bay)

Amlwch

9

Cemaes

8 7

10

11

5 Moelfr

Caergybi
(Holyhead)

Môn
Anglesey

12 14

Walk 11
Melin Llynnon

Walk details

Approx distance: *4 miles/6.4 kilometres*

Approx time: *1½ hours*

O.S. Maps: *1:50 000 Landranger Sheet 114*
1:25 000 Explorer Sheet 262

Start: *Melin Llynnon*
Grid Ref. SH 340 852

Access: *B5109 west of Trefor / A5025 south of Llanfaethlu.*
Entering Llanddeusant, there is a brown sign at the
crossroads directing you to Melin Llynnon.
Two buses each day from Amlwch and Holyhead
pass through Llanddeusant.

Parking: *Large parking at the Mill.*

Please note: *Fields may be wet after heavy rainfall.*
The lane from Howell Water Mill is poor, and could
be muddy after heavy rainfall.

Going: *Lanes / tarmac road / quiet / muddy.*
Lanes and fields.

Points of Interest

1. After 60 years of disuse the windmill at Melin Llynnon was finally restored and opened to the public in 1984. At one time there were more than 150 windmills in Wales, many of them on Anglesey, an ideal place to utilize wind power.

The first windmills were the post-mills. The whole

*The beautifully restored Melin Llynnon
and one of the Celtic roundhouses*

mill structure, a wooden box on posts, could be turned to face the wind. Sails drove millstones but they were dangerous and could not be controlled. By the 16th century the round, straight-sided, stone tower mills had taken over. With the aid of a pole, their caps (tops) could be rotated to move the sails into the wind. About 200 years later, the towers became tapering and taller, raising the cap and sails to catch more wind. In Anglesey, the Penmon and Benllech quarries produced good quality mill-stones. Melin Llynnon was built in 1776 and the first miller, Thomas Jones, was 90 when he died. The tenancy passed to his descendants but the repeal of the Corn Laws in 1846 led to a decline in the use of windmills and this mill became disused by 1923.

Storms damaged the cap allowing water to enter the mill. Anglesey Borough Council purchased Melin Llynnon in 1978 and restoration was carried out by specialist millwrights from Lincolnshire.

2. Llantrisant Old Church is at present looked after by the Friends of Friendless Churches. Built in the 14th century it is dedicated to St Afran, St Ieuan and St Sannan. The south chapel was added later in the 17th century. The church has some interesting 17th and 18th century memorials and 19th-century box pews.

3. In the Middle Ages there were over 60 mills on Anglesey including one here close to Afon Alaw. The early mills would have been quite small, consisting of a water-wheel driving a set of stones, some storage space and a place to dry grain. The present mill, Howell Mill, was enlarged in 1850 on the upstream side. Restoration work was carried out about 100 years later and the mill won a conservation award. The leat is fed by a dammed section of Afon Alaw upstream which forms a small reservoir. This mill has survived but most water-mills closed when it was realised that windmills provided a more reliable source of energy on Anglesey. Water-mills require a constant supply of water, which could not be guaranteed in dry summers.

4. The barrow, Bedd Branwen, is traditionally associated with Branwen, daughter of Llŷr, whose story is told in the collection of classical Welsh tales known as the Mabinogion. In the story Branwen marries Matholwch, King of Ireland, and the wedding feast is celebrated at Aberffraw. Her half-brother Efnisien is angry when he finds out that Branwen has married

without his consent and he mutilates Matholwch's horses. Branwen and her husband sail to Ireland but, because of the insult, she is soon forced to work in the kitchen. She rears a starling, teaches it to speak, and after three years sends the bird to Wales with news of her misery. Her brother Bendigeidfran sails to Ireland and in the ensuing battle only 7 men from the 'Island of the Mighty' (the land of the Brythonic people) survive. Branwen and the 7 return home with the head of Bendigeidfran. They land on the west coast of Anglesey and as they sit and rest, Branwen looks towards Ireland and the Island of the Mighty. Because of the trouble she has caused, she regrets being born. On the bank of the Alaw she dies of a broken heart and they bury her there. The Mabinogion was written in the 11th century – Aberffraw was then the chief court of the Princes of Gwynedd. However, the story may include an earlier oral tradition.

Excavation has revealed that the barrow was built in the Bronze Age as a communal burial place. At the centre there is a large stone which may have been a monument long beforehand. An urn with bones was found early in the 19th century. When full excavation took place about 30 years ago several urns containing cremated bones and imported beads were uncovered. The site appears to have been used at different periods with two sets of burials. Beside some of the urns there were accessory pots (smaller pots) containing ear bones of newborn babies, suggestive of some kind of ritual. To reach the site follow the track across a cattle grid. Shortly before the track bends left at some woods, there is a field gate on the right. Although the land is private, if the land is not being used for crops or hay, access is usually allowed to the monument. Slant

Inside Howell Mill

right across the field for some distance. The low barrow with its central stone is in a bend of Afon Alaw.

Walk directions (-) **denotes Point of Interest**
Starting from the car park at Melin Llynnon (1) turn left on the lane. At the crossroads keep ahead on the lane signposted Trefor.

The lane crosses Afon Alaw and passes a house with a large white gate on the right called New Hafren. Look for a narrow lane on the left. This is taken after visiting Llantrisant Old Church.

To visit the church, continue 100 metres to a stone stile on the right. Follow the right edge of the field, keep ahead through a gate and pass a farm on the left. Cross a stile in the left corner and turn right through a gate to the church (2).

Millstones at Howell Mill

From the church return the same way to the lane. Turn left then right on the narrow lane seen earlier. Follow it to Howell Mill (3).

With the mill on the right, follow the rough lane uphill. It bends right to a wider lane at Elim.

Turn left for about 400 metres to a track on the right for Glan Alaw. Bedd Branwen lies in a field off this track (4).

Continue on the lane. The lane bends left past houses to a junction. Cross the road directly to a track.

Follow the track and where it bends right go through the second of two gates on the left. Follow the wall and hedge on the left. Cross a rough stile into the next field.

Continue to a stile on the left of the church ahead. Follow an enclosed path to the road in Llanddeusant village.

Turn right and at the crossroads turn right again to the start at Melin Llynnon.

Facilities
Tea-room and toilets at Melin Llynnon. The mill is open April to September. Closed on Mondays.

Originally published in
Circular Walks on Anglesey

by Dorothy Hamilton

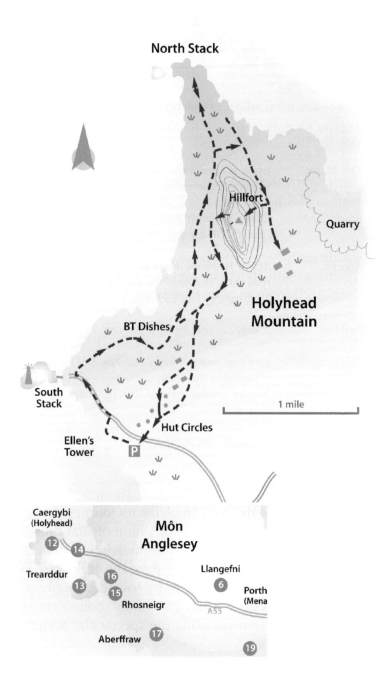

Walk 12

Mynydd Tŵr, Caergybi

Walk details

Approx distance: *4 miles/6.4 kilometres*

Approx time:	*2 hours*
O.S. Maps:	*1:50 000 Landranger Sheet 114* *1:25 000 Explorer Sheet 262*
Start:	*Ellen's Tower car park* *Grid Ref. SH 211 819*
Access:	*A55 to Holyhead. From the High Street follow the road out of Holyhead towards Holyhead Mountain. Turn right by the RSPB sign.*
Parking:	*A large car park by the RSPB sign.*
Please note:	*Very high and dangerous paths around the summit of Holyhead Mountain.* *Marshy ground between the lighthouse and the Telecom dishes.*
Going:	*Cliff walks and marshy ground.*

It is at Holyhead (*Caergybi*) that Thomas Telford's great road, now the A5, completes its journey. It was finished in 1826 after the Act of Union of 1821 caused the need for improved communications between London and Dublin. In those days the trek took in excess of 40 hours in what must have been extreme discomfort, inside a cold, noisy and bone-shaking stagecoach. After negotiating the spectacular scenery

The view from Mynydd Twr

of Snowdonia the weary travellers would have welcomed the bleak, seemingly flat countryside of Anglesey for it heralded the last leg of the journey.

This sudden change of landscape is somewhat surprising for across the narrow Menai Strait the mountains tower so impressively. If beautiful countryside is to be found on Anglesey, then it is on the coastline rather than its interior.

Our walk concentrates on one of the most attractive parts of that coastline, Mynydd Caergybi (*Holyhead Mountain*). At a mere 722 feet (220m) it is perhaps optimistic to call it a mountain but nevertheless there are many fine views from its summit. The area is also an RSPB reserve, one of the largest in the country.

South Stack lighthouse

A Twitcher's Paradise

We leave the upper car park near South Stack (*Ynys Lawd*) and head for Ellen's Tower. Once a summerhouse, it is now an RSPB visitor centre where binoculars and telescopes are provided for scanning the cliffs. Puffins, guillemots, razorbills, fulmars and the very rare chough breed on South Stack and attract many ornithologists here.

Nearby is South Stack kitchen, open for refreshments from Easter to September.

We can now descent to South Stack itself, a pear-shaped island connected to the mainland by a chain suspension bridge. The lighthouse is open to the public during the summer. Having descended the 160 steps to the bridge, if equipped with a North Wales Nature Trust leaflet, you can follow the nature trail, each point having the corresponding numbers on the wall. Cliff plants abound on the rocks including spring squill, stonecrop, campion, sheep's bit, golden samphire and restharrow. Even more importantly, maritime field fleawort flowers here in May and June, this being the only place in the world where it is found. The rock is also home to many lichens which are a good indication that this is a pollution free area.

The conditions also attract a wide variety of songbirds in addition to the seabirds. Wheatears, warblers and whinchats are common in spring and autumn and the rarer honey buzzard, bee-eater, dotterel and red-footed falcon have also been seen.

For the Safety of Shipping
We continue over the cliffs to North Stack where there is a Fog Signal Station equipped with an isolated magazine for storing the distress flares away from the main building. As a further reminder of how treacherous these waters can be we can see the Skerries rocks away to the north complete with their own lighthouse to warn shipping away.

Returning to the north-eastern side of Holyhead Mountain gives us a fine view over the harbour. Connections with Ireland date back to 2000 BC, with an early trade in axes, but the town remained a fishing village until the development stimulated by the Act of Union. The great breakwater sheltering the harbour was a mammoth project. It was started in 1847 by James Rendal and was taken over in 1856 by John Hawkshaw for Rendal died long before its final completion in 1873.

The stone was quarried from Holyhead Mountain and was being dumped in the sea at 24,000 tonnes per week. It is only when one considers that the whole structure is 1.8 miles (2.9km) long and some 40 feet (12m) above low water that its size is fully appreciated.

A hut circle on Mynydd Caergybi

Ferries for Ireland, both the hydrofoil and conventional type, are seen making frequent crossings.

An Ancient Hillfort
As we ascend the mountain we come to another major building project but from a much earlier time. Caer-y-twr is an Iron Age hillfort enclosing an area of 17 acres (7 hectares) just below the summit. The path passes through an entrance between two rock outcrops flanked by the jumbled remains of the rock walls. It was built to protect the inhabitants from Irish raiders in AD 200-400.

At the summit of the mountain the Triangulation Point adjoins the foundations of a Roman lighthouse.

Neolithic Hut Circles
As the walk nears its completion there is a final point of interest at Cytiau'r Gwyddelod, a collection of 20 hut circles dating back to the Neolithic, Early Bronze

The path on Mynydd Twr

Age of 2000 BC. They were occupied through to
Roman times and after. The building of these
structures was spread over a one thousand year period
and comprise of eight farmsteads with their adjoining
stores and workshops. It appears that only one or two
were occupied at any one time. Excavations show that
the Bronze Age diet was largely grain supplemented by
limpets, for crushed shells were found in considerable
quantities.

The walk
Start at the upper (first) car park for Ellen's Tower on
the minor road leading from Holyhead to South Stack
(Grid Ref. SH 211 818).

1. Take the footpath signposted for Ellen's Tower
Information Centre.
   From the tower climb the steps and continue along
the cliff path following it up to a stone wall and the
road. Turn left down the road to the entrance of South
Stack lighthouse.

2. Now continue along the waymarked path, passing a
stone shelter and on along the cliffs passing radio
masts to the right. Bear left along a tarmac road and off
to the right behind the Telecom dishes. Keep bearing
left between two rocky summits and then right on to
the ridge leading down to North Stack. Continue along
the ridge to overlook North Stack and the Fog Warning
Station.

3. Retrace your steps heading towards Mynydd Twr
(*Holyhead Mountain*) with the Triangulation Pillar
visible on top. As the path starts to climb up the far

Ellen's Tower

side of the saddle look out for a narrow track sharp left. Follow it to a fine view over Holyhead Harbour. It will lead to a T-junction with a cliff top path. Turn right keeping the harbour views on your left. Continue until the hillside flattens out. Now take a small path right that is heading towards the summit of Holyhead Mountain. The path widens and meanders up the hillside. As it begins to climb more steeply it passes between two rocks with adjoining walls that formed the entrance to Caer-y-tŵr, an Iron Age fort. Continue to the summit.

4. The route from the summit is extremely steep, most definitely not recommended for young children or anyone unsure of their balance. At best it is a steep scramble. You may prefer to retrace your steps and make your way round the hilltop. Whichever way you descend the point you need to make for is the path running along the foot of the escarpment.

The best way down the steep section is to head for the Telecom dishes from the summit. Here rough steps lead down the scramble. About 70 yards (65m) from the base of the steps a track leads off to the left. This is the path leading along the base of the escarpment. Follow it inland until it meets a wider track at a T-junction overlooking a rectangular reservoir. Turn right back towards the Telecom dishes but shortly take a narrow path left heading towards a lone radio mast. This passes behind some cottages and then right along a grassy lane. It then joins a tarmac and stony lane. Now keep your eyes open to the left for a narrow path leading into the area of stone hut circles, Cytiau'r Gwyddelod. Exit from the circles through a gate on to the road opposite the car park entrance.

Originally published in
Family Walks to Discover North Wales

by Anna & Graham Francis

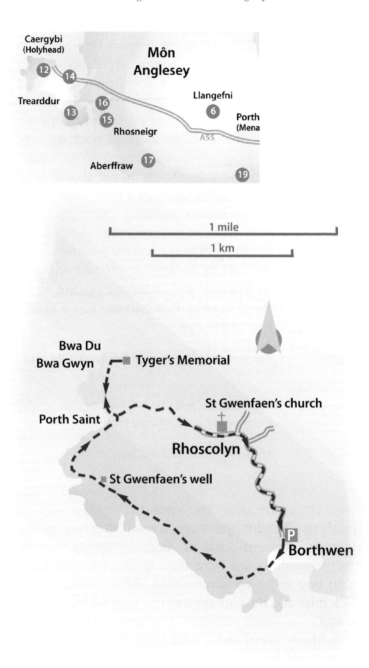

Walk 13
Rhoscolyn

Walk details
Approx distance: *5 miles/8 kilometres*

Approx time: *1½ hours*

O.S. Maps: *1:50 000 Landranger Sheet 114*
               1:25 000 Explorer Sheet 262

Start: *Borthwen Beach*
        Grid Ref. SH 273 753

Access: *A55 Holyhead / B4545 Trearddur-Rhoscolyn.*
        On the B4545 to Trearddur, take the left turning
        towards Rhoscolyn.

Parking: *Car park by the beach, or by the church if the beach*
        is full.

Please note: *Cliff walks and fields.*
        Fields can get muddy during winter.

Going: *Moderate – beach, cliff and lanes.*

Tyger the Brave Dog – the legend

Nearly two hundred years ago, a small ship was sailing along the western coast of Anglesey on its way to Liverpool. On board were the captain, two sailors, a cabin boy and a retriever called Tyger. There was a thick mist and the captain was not sure where exactly he was.

Suddenly, there was a loud bang. The ship had hit the rocks of Maen Pisgar, a small island about ¾ of a mile offshore. As the ship was not sinking, nothing could be done, so the captain decided to wait for the mist to lift.

The tide came in and lifted the ship off the rocks, but as there was a hole in its keel, the water started to flow in, and the ship started to sink. The thick mist was around them and the crew were not sure in which direction to swim for the shore.

Tyger had also realised that they were in danger. But he knew in which direction the coast was and he jumped into the sea and started swimming. The captain decided that the crew should follow Tyger and they all jumped into the sea.

The captain was a strong swimmer, but the others weren't. The cabin boy grabbed hold of Tyger's collar and he was dragged slowly to the pebbly beach. The captain then realised that one of the sailors was in difficulty, so after Tyger had left the cabin boy safely on the beach, he asked Tyger to return to help the sailor.

Tyger returned and grabbed hold of the sailor's collar with his teeth and dragged him to the shore. The dog then returned to help the other sailor and then his master, the captain.

All five lay very tired and wet on the beach. One by one, they got up – but not Tyger. He was too tired. He raised his head and licked the captain's hand before dying on the cold, wet beach.

If it had not been for Tyger's bravery, they would have all drowned. And in order to show his appreciation of his brave dog, the captain paid for a stone to be placed on the cliff above the beach where all four landed safely and where Tyger had died.

And the stone is still there, and on it the words: 'Tyger, Sep. 17th, 1819'.

The Tyger memorial stone

The walk

Go to the village of Rhoscolyn and look for the church. About a hundred feet to the west of the church you will see a sign to the beach. It is possible to reach Rhoscolyn by bus, but you will then have to walk to the church and start your walk from here. Go down to the beach where there is a car park and toilets. It can be very full here in summer, and you may find parking space by the church; you can then start the walk from there.

At Borthwen, walk to the right to a wall and path. Follow the path which brings you back to the beach. Then go past the old lifeboat house. Go up the hill to the white house where you will see yellow signs pointing to the right towards a house called Yr Allt.

Then go straight ahead along the shore, past the coastguard look-out station on your left and another look-out and bench on your right. After a while you will reach St Gwenfaen's Well, where, they say, if you throw

Rhoscolyn and Borthwen

two white stones into its waters, you will be cured of any mental illness.

Carry on along the path, through a kissing gate, and along the path that runs alongside a high wall. You will then reach Porth Saint. Cross the small footbridge and continue along the path. Now, you should see a large white house in front of you; there is no need for you to go as far as there. After you pass a small bay, you will see five stones on your left. The first of these is Tyger's memorial stone. When the tide is out, you can see Maen Pisgar out at sea where the ship was wrecked.

After a rest, turn back for Porth Saint. To the left you will see a stile, go over it and along the field to another stile. Then follow the old track until you reach the farmhouse. Follow the yellow signs around the house until you come to a kissing gate and Public Footpath sign. Go through the gate, then to the left and along the road until you reach St Gwenfaen's church. Why not go and see the church? Then look for the sign

Traeth Llydan, Rhoscolyn

to the beach. Walk down the road, past the pub, and along the winding road back to the car park.

Originally published in
Walking Adventures on Anglesey

by Dafydd Meirion

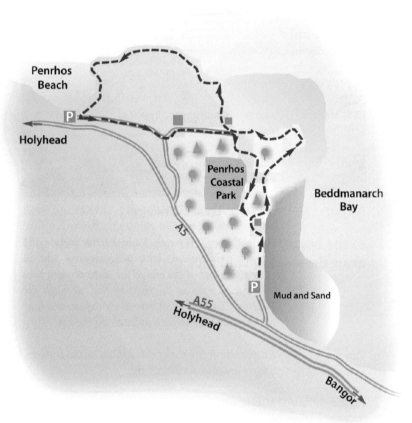

Walk 14
Penrhos Coastal Park

Walk details
Approx distance: *3½ miles/5.6 kilometre*

Approx time:	*2 hours*
O.S. Maps:	*1:50 000 Landranger Sheet 114* *1:25 000 Explorer Sheet 262*
Start:	*Penrhos Coastal car park* *Grid Ref. SH 275 805*
Access:	*Leave the A55 at the Valley exit. Take the A5 north towards Valley, and at the traffic lights, continue straight ahead through Valley. Drive across the Stanley Embankment with Beddmanarch Bay on your right, and at the end of the embankment, take the first turning on the right by the toll house for Penrhos Coastal Park. Drive down the narrow lane and park in the car park overlooking the bay.*
Parking:	*Purpose-built car park for Penrhos Coastal walkers. Toilets and café facilities here.*
Please note:	*Muddy paths in the trees.*
Going:	*A pleasant coastal walk.* *A very relaxing walk, where you can spot a lot of wildlife lurking in the surrounding trees and bushes.*

Site highlights
- Easy walking in attractive coastal scenery.
- Mix of estuarine and woodland walking and birding.

Penrhos Coastal Park

Walk description

This is an easy circular walk offering attractive views across the bay and a variety of habitat from coastal to woodland. As a result you can enjoy a variety of birdlife too, from waders and gulls in Beddmanarch Bay, to woodland birds and summer migrants in the grounds of the former grand estate here. Although the car park at Penrhos Coastal Park may be busy, a short walk down the path will soon take you away from the crowds and you can enjoy the peaceful scenery by yourself.

Walk directions

Before heading off on your walk, take time to scan the bay, ideally with a telescope. This is the widest part of the waterway that technically separates Holy Island from the rest of Anglesey. The shallows here mean that the tide advances and retreats a long way, and rapidly, here. At low tide, the mudflats are exposed and you should see a good range of waders including

Oystercatchers, Ringed Plovers, Curlews, and in season, Whimbrels, Bar-tailed and Black-tailed Godwits. Pale-bellied Brent Geese often congregate here in winter, and it is always worth checking the gull flocks to see if you can pick out something unusual amongst the Common, Herring, and Black-headed regulars. Look further out across the water with your telescope in winter, and you may be rewarded with Great Northern Divers and Slavonian Grebes, as well as the more regular Great Crested Grebes, Cormorants and Red-breasted Mergansers.

From the car park, take the metalled path past the toilet block on your left, and continue onwards keeping the bay on your right until you reach Beddmanarch House after about ¼ mile/0.4 km. The path turns inland here to circuit the house and you need to turn right past a wooden gate. You shortly reach the site of a Pet Cemetery, where you turn right following the Anglesey Coastal Path until you are back at the shore again. Turn left and walk past the bench and shelter. A bit further along, you will pass 'Tunnicliffe's Seat' on your right. On reaching a patch of open grass, you may wish to check the small pond on your left for duck and Grey Heron, while, in summer, warblers may be lurking in the surrounding bushes. Just past this point the path splits. Take the right-hand path, still following the Anglesey Coastal Path, which leads you out into an open area of traditionally-managed meadowland. Walk to the top of the hill and enjoy the views from the top of Gorsedd-y-penrhyn of Beddmanarch Bay to your right, and Holyhead Harbour and Holyhead Mountain in the distance to your left. A thoughtfully-placed stone seat means you can admire the view in either direction.

Butterflies such as Clouded Yellow, Tortoiseshell, and Peacock are attracted in summer to the wildflowers in this area of unspoiled meadowland which is managed by Anglesey Aluminium who bought the Penrhos Estate in 1972. Check the bushes all around this area for summer migrants: Lesser and Common Whitethroats can be found here, Blackcaps, Garden Warblers and Grasshopper Warblers can be heard (if not seen) here too. Scanning across towards the Alaw estuary, you may be able to add to your list of waders, while you may see Cormorants and terns flying past the point as you look out to sea. Facing towards Holyhead Harbour, you may see in the distance one of the ferries or the catamaran that crosses to Ireland from here.

From here, head back down the other side of the flower meadow and take the small path on the right down on to the beach. Turn left and follow the sandy beach round towards the white house, following the footpath back up into the trees by the red lifebelt, just before you reach the house.

The area of Penrhos Coastal Path was the estate of the Stanley family from 1763. Apparently this area used to be their private beach, and in later years the building here served as a 'beach hut'.

Walk past a wooden gate and along the lane for a very short distance before taking the footpath on your right, signposted the Anglesey Coastal Path. Follow this path for about ¾ mile/1.2 km as it winds its way along the cliff, past the ruins of what used to be a boathouse, and 'The Battery'.

Follow the yellow footpath markers as the path descends through the dunes towards a car park. As you reach the lane, turn left and walk past some houses. At the junction, continue straight ahead through the stone gateway towards Penrhos Farm, following the blue footpath marker. Pass the cricket pitch on your left (keeping an eye out for Mistle Thrushes and Pied Wagtails strutting about on its tended lawn) and continue towards the farm. When you reach the buildings, bear left towards Penrhos Farm, passing 'The Tower' on your right and keeping the cricket pitch on your left, following the blue footpath marker. Pass a square tower on your left and walk straight across an open yard, keeping some old buildings on your right. Go through a wooden gate marked 'Beach House' and walk down the lane still following the blue footpath marker. You will soon reach the white house again, but this time, turn right to pass into the woods through the gate in the stone wall.

These woods are a real joy in May, when the leaves are still in their bright green colouring, and the floor is carpeted with bluebells and wild garlic. The scent is heavenly as you walk along, and the trees are not leaved so thickly that you cannot, with some persistence, see the birds that are singing around you: Chiffchaffs, Willow Warblers, Garden Warblers, Blackcaps, Song Thrushes, Blackbirds, Robins and Wrens. As well as wildlife, these woodlands are reputed to be home to a number of ghosts too: one, who has been seen by a number of people is that of a German parachutist who is supposed to have bailed out of his damaged aircraft only to be killed upon landing in the woods. There are no historical records to support this story, but nevertheless, keep your eyes peeled for an unusual sight in the trees!

Turn right by the footpath sign to walk towards an ornamental column. Continue past this straight ahead to walk through a gap in the high wall.

The old walls and stone steps that you can just make out here suggest that this was once part of a more formal garden. Some rhododendrons and spotted laurels grow here, and in May the air is heady with the scent of the wild garlic at your feet.

Turn left at a yellow footpath marker just before a bench and take the right fork past a stone wall. The footpath takes a meandering route to bring you back through a gap in the high wall out onto a wider path. Turn right here and walk through a tunnel of trees. Turn left by a yellow footpath marker at the corner of a stone wall on your left, and walk past the ruins of some mini 'ramparts'. Keeping the stone wall on your left, continue straight ahead at a crossroads of footpaths. At the next crossroads amongst some conifer trees, continue straight ahead again, listening carefully for any Coal Tits or Goldfinches in the area. Crossing a wooden bridge over a stream, you reach the pet cemetery once again. Turn right, pass a wooden gate and then turn left to get back to the water's edge and your route back to the car park.

If birds or wild flowers tempt you to wander down alternative paths through the woodland, don't worry. There are many paths to take here, and providing you keep the slight traffic noise from the main road on your right, you can't go far wrong.

What to look for ...
... in spring: Pale-bellied Brent Geese and Slavonian Grebes may be seen out on the water up until the end of April, by which time the Grebes may be looking

particularly fine in their breeding plumage, as well as Great Northern Divers. Look out also for passage waders such as Bar-tailed Godwits and Whimbrels, Dunlins, Knots and Sanderlings. In late spring and summer, the woodland and parkland areas are likely to be resounding with the songs of warblers such as Willow Warblers, Chiffchaffs, Common and Lesser Whitethroats, reeling Grasshopper Warblers, and who knows, maybe a rarity might drop in.

... in summer: Look offshore when you're walking along the coastal cliffs for terns, usually Common or Sandwich Terns, but if you're lucky, you may also catch sight of an Arctic Tern. Keep checking the woodland and hedgerow areas in early summer for warblers, as well as woodland regulars such as mixed tit flocks.

... in autumn: Passage waders are likely to be passing through again, using the exposed mudflats of the bay as a stopping off point. Look out for Bar-tailed Godwits, Knots, Whimbrels, Sanderlings, Dunlins and Grey Plovers.

... in winter: Brent Geese will be returning to the bay again, as will Slavonian and Great Crested Grebes and Great Northern Divers. Bar-tailed Godwits, Knots, Dunlins and Grey Plovers may also still be here, particularly outside high tide. In cold weather, this can be a good place to do your birdwatching from the warmth and comfort from your car in the car park.

... all year round: You should be able to see a variety of gulls, Red-breasted Mergansers, and waders such as Oystercatchers, Ringed Plovers, Cormorants and

Dullin flock

Curlews here all year round, particularly when the tide is falling and the mudflats are exposed.

Where to eat
The Toll House is situated at the entrance to the car park of Penrhos Coast Park and it has an interesting history. As the Stanley Tollhouse, it was originally located next to the Telford Road at the Holyhead end of the embankment. However, in the 1960s it had to be moved by Anglesey County Council to make way for a water main in connection with the Anglesey Aluminium smelting plant up the road. The entire tollhouse was dismantled stone by stone and rebuilt slightly further down the road in its present position. Each side of the building was painted in two different colours and each stone numbered in sequence to ensure it was all put back together again in the right order!

Cafés can be found at the village of Valley, just five minutes away by car, down the A5 heading south towards the A55. At the traffic lights, turn right and park in the car park on the left. There are a couple of good cafés here: Caffi Arian on the main Station Road, and Café Milano off the car park itself.

Other information
- Free car park.
- Public toilets on site.

What other sights are nearby
- Holyhead Harbour, and Breakwater Country Park.
- South Stack RSPB Reserve.
- Anglesey Coastal Path.

Originally published in
Birds, Boots and Butties – Anglesey

by Ruth Miller

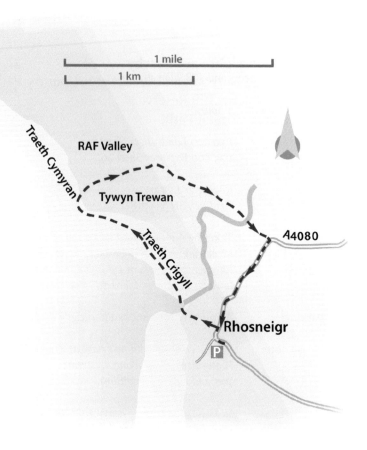

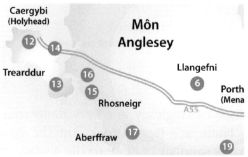

Walk 15
The Wreckers of Crigyll, Rhosneigr

Walk details
Approx distance: *5 miles /8 kilometres*

Approx time: *2 hours*

O.S. Maps: *1:50 000 Landranger Sheet 114*
1:25 000 Explorer Sheet 262

Start: *Rhosneigr Library*
Grid Ref. SH 332 718

Access: *Take the A4080 to Rhosneigr. Turn left by the War Memorial with a clock on top, in the centre of Rhosneigr. Then turn left again, following the sign towards Rhosneigr Library.*

Parking: *A large free car park by Rhosneigr Library.*

Please note: *Stream crossing with no bridge at Traeth Crigyll. Footbridge further along up stream. Wet and marshy conditions.*

WARNING: During heavy rain, the sea comes in very close, and the river floods the land surrounding the footbridge – I speak from experience!!

Going: *Quiet / muddy. Beach, sand dunes and lanes.*

The Wreckers of Crigyll – the legend
The coast of Anglesey is a very dangerous place for ships. There are jagged rocks on the coastline and dangerous sandbanks close to the surface, and during

Traeth Crigyll

stormy weather ships can be blown onto the shore. Two centuries ago, there were people who were more than happy to see ships being blown onto the beaches so that they could steal their cargoes.

There was such a group of people living near Traeth Crigyll in Rhosneigr. It is said that the Wreckers of Crigyll would wave their lamps on the beach so that ships thought it was safe to come ashore. Traeth Crigyll was a good place for the wreckers to live. There were rocks offshore and lots of sand dunes where they could hide, as well as frequent mists to hide their evil deeds.

One stormy night in December 1741, a ship called *Loveday and Betty* was sailing off the coast of Anglesey. But the following morning she was thrown onto the rocks near the mouth of Afon Crigyll. She had not suffered much damage, apart from scraping her keel on the rocks.

Captain Jackson from Liverpool made sure that his ship was safely anchored and then went to fetch help

A scene at Beaumaris court

to get the ship back into the water. But news of the ship on the shore quickly spread throughout the area, and after it got dark ten local men went to the beach. They first took the sails, then the ropes and carried them to the horses that were waiting in the dunes to carry them away.

When the captain returned, he saw that there were many things missing from his ship and he decided to go to Aberffraw to look for the customs officer to report the theft. Both returned to Traeth Crigyll on horseback and decided to follow the tracks of the wreckers through the sand dunes. They galloped after the wreckers and eventually caught up with them and captured four of them.

On 7 April, 1741, the wreckers were tried in the court in Beaumaris. There was a great deal of interest in the case, and many people travelled from afar to see the trial, hoping that all four would be hanged. But the judge was drunk and he decided to free the four wreckers!

Before then, in April 1715, three of the Crigyll Wreckers had been brought to court for stealing goods from a ship called *The Charming Jenny* which had also been blown onto the beach. These were not so fortunate – they were all hanged. This was the first time that people had heard of the Wreckers of Crigyll.

The stealing continued for another century. There was one famous case towards the end of October 1867 when goods were stolen from a ship called *Earl of Chester*. According to a report in *The Times* newspaper, 'there were hundreds of them carrying everything from the ship'.

But by today, Traeth Crigyll is a very peaceful place with sailing boats and children building sandcastles where once wreckers lurked waiting for ships to go on the rocks.

The walk
Park your car in the free car park near the library and toilets in Rhosneigr and then walk down the hill. Turn right and then go along the main street. If you are travelling by bus, there is a bus stop here. Walk towards the war memorial with the clock on top.

Then turn left and go down the hill to the beach. Turn right and walk along the sands until you come to the mouth of Afon Crigyll. You will have to take your shoes and socks off to cross it. If you don't want to get your feet wet, walk up river to a footbridge and then return to the beach. The vast stretch of sand ahead of you is Traeth Crigyll where the wreckers carried out their evil deeds.

Walk to the far end of Traeth Crigyll; around the corner is Traeth Cymyran (where it is said that Madam Wen's ship was anchored – see Walk 16). Walk for a few yards on Traeth Cymyran, but then look for a path that goes up into the dunes. Go up into the dunes and before you is RAF Valley with its hangars and landing strips. It is possible that you will see aircraft landing and taking off, and it is quite possible that you will have heard them in the skies after reaching Rhosneigr.

Look for a small fence that goes across Tywyn Trewan. There are signs warning you not to go onto the airfield land. Follow the path that runs alongside the fence.

Then, near a high fence the path turns right. Follow this path and although it turns left further along, walk straight ahead aiming for the footbridge. Go over the footbridge and up the lane to a cluster of houses. The lane goes past the houses and takes you to a large square building. Turn left near this building and then into the main road. Turn right and walk back into the village.

Originally published in
Walking Adventures on Anglesey

by Dafydd Meirion

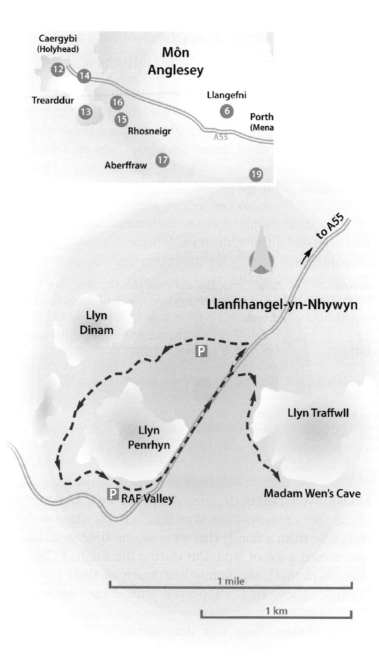

Walk 16
Madam Wen, the Welsh Highwaywoman

Walk details
Approx distance: *4 miles /6.4 kilometres*

Approx time:	*1½ hours*
O.S. Maps:	*1:50 000 Landranger Sheet 114* *1:25 000 Explorer Sheet 262*
Start:	*Llanfihangel-yn-Nhywyn* *Grid Ref. SH 322 775*
Access:	*Take Caergeiliog exit from the A55, then turn left towards Llanfihangel-yn-Nhywyn. Park by the church.*
Parking:	*Car park by roadside in front of shops.*
Please note:	*Wet land by lakes – especially after heavy rain.*
Going:	*Lakeside / quiet.* *Lakeside and lanes – easy.*

Madam Wen, the Welsh Highwaywoman – the legend
Madam Wen lived in the lakes district of west Anglesey in the 18th century. Einir Wyn was her real name and she came from a family that were at one time wealthy and owned a lot of land. But during the English Civil War (1642-1651), the family lost much of their lands because they had supported the King against Parliament.

But Madam Wen was determined to get some money to buy these lands back. She gathered together

Llyn Traffwll

a gang of men who went robbing and smuggling on Anglesey. Madam Wen had one of the best horses on Anglesey and could outrun everyone, and she only travelled at night galloping as fast as her horse could take her.

The authorities did not know who was responsible for all the robberies and smuggling on the island and when they did come across Madam Wen they could not catch her. Madam Wen and her gang used to hide in a cave near Llyn Traffwll and since the entrance was hidden by very thick and high gorse bushes it was impossible to find them.

One night, with snow thick on the ground, Madam Wen and her gang went to hold up the stagecoach. But the authorities were watching the coach and they galloped after Madam Wen and her gang. They were determined to catch her, but one of the gang, Wil the blacksmith, had a brainwave. He took the horseshoes off Madam Wen's horse and put them back on back-to-front. The authorities, rather than following Madam Wen's horse tracks in the snow, were going in the direction that she had come from!

Madam Wen and her gang would also smuggle goods into Anglesey. It is said that she had a ship anchored off Cymyran Bay, and her gang would carry the smuggled goods to be sold all over the island. As people were not paying taxes on these goods, the authorities were very angry and they were very keen to catch Madam Wen – but they always failed.

Only one member of the gang was ever caught – Wil the blacksmith. He had gone to Menai Bridge fair and was about to start off home when he put someone else's saddle on his horse in mistake. He was accused of stealing the saddle and dragged to the court, found guilty and fined. Wil was so embarrassed by being caught for something so petty, and he having stolen so much over the years, that he emigrated to America to live!

But Madam Wen did eventually become the owner of much land – but not her family's lands. Einir Wyn married Morris Williams, owner of the Cymunod estate, and both lived happily ever after with very few people knowing that she had been Madam Wen.

Some people say that they have seen the ghost of Madam Wen in the lakes, especially on Easter Sunday morning. It is said that she swims backwards and forwards and then when she reaches the middle, she disappears!

The walk
Go through Ffordd Cerrig Mawr housing estate and at the far end you will see a Public Footpath sign. Go down the track to a small house. To the left is a kissing gate, go through it and keep to the right-hand side of

Llanfihangel-yn-Nhywyn

the field until you come to another kissing gate. Go through it and then go straight ahead – don't turn right.

Then, at the far end of the field, turn right and walk towards a stile. Go over it and across the next field to a stile near a gate. Go over it and follow the path with Llyn Penrhyn on your left until you come to another stile near a gate. Go over it and along the field with the lake and rock to your left. If you climb to the top of the rock, you will see Llyn Dinam on the right.

Look for a pole with a yellow arrow on it behind clumps of gorse. There is a path near it; turn left and then go over a bridge made of wooden planks and on to another one. Follow the path between two rocks, keeping to the left or go over one of the rocks if it is too wet and then follow the path through the gorse.

You will then come to a footbridge, go over it and follow the path until you come to three poles with lamps on them on your right. The path goes past the third pole and then you will see more lamps on your left. You will then come to a track and then to a row of lamps on a fence.

Walk towards a gate and stile, go through the gate and continue along the path to the Valley Lakes Nature Reserve car park. Go out of the car park near the RAF Valley entrance and then turn left, walking along the pavement back to Llanfihangel-yn-Nhywyn where the journey started.

Madam Wen's Cave is near Llyn Traffwll – why not try and find it? On the way back to Llanfihangel-yn-Nhywyn after passing RAF Valley, you will see Bryn Trewan housing estate on your right. Turn into the estate and walk until you come to a junction. Turn right and go down a narrow lane. Before you come to an agricultural building, you will see a muddy track going towards a gate. In the corner, near a tree, there is an old stile on the right (it is a bit difficult to find).

Go over the stile and across the field, aiming for a gate in the far end. To the left of the gate is an iron stile. You will now see Llyn Traffwll to the left and some large rocks in front of you. Somewhere in these rocks is Madam Wen's Cave. Go over the stile and walk along the shore of the lake through the rocks and gorse bushes until you come to a flat field on the lake shore. Before reaching this field, there is a large rock with a huge crack in it. This is Madam Wen's Cave. Some say that there is a secret room beneath it. Can you find it?

Originally published in
Walking Adventures on Anglesey

by Dafydd Meirion

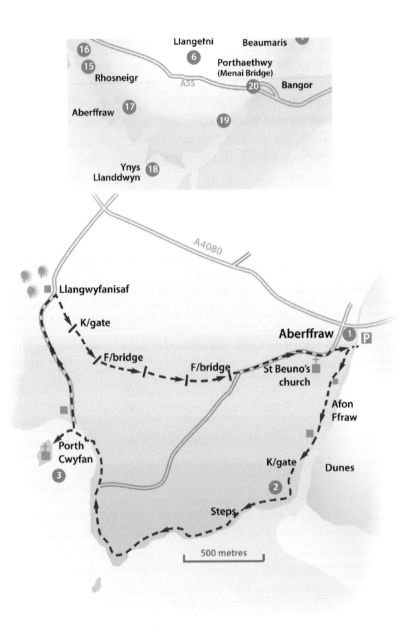

Walk 17
Aberffraw

Walk details
Approx distance: *4½ miles/7.2 kilometres*

Approx time:	*3 hours*
O.S. Maps:	*1:50 000 Landranger Sheet 114* *1:25 000 Explorer Sheet 262*
Start:	*At the old bridge, Grid Ref. SH 356 689*
Access:	*Take the A4080 from Menai Bridge. Aberffraw is 6 miles west of Newborough. Just before Aberffraw turn left on a minor road. Buses from Bangor, Llangefni and Holyhead.*
Parking:	*Car park near the road at the old bridge.*
Please note:	*Moderate cliff height.* *Fields could be wet in the winter.* *Porth Cwyfan can be very rocky to walk on.*
Going:	*Lanes, low cliff paths and fields.*

Points of Interest
1. Aberffraw was the main court of the Princes of Gwynedd from the 6th–13th centuries and from here they ruled all of northern Wales. Nothing remains of the timber palace although it survived Edward I's invasion. Later, in 1317 it was demolished and used in the construction of Caernarfon castle. The court (*llys*) was probably situated in the older part of Aberffraw village. Excavation west of Bodorgan Square revealed

The old bridge, Aberffraw

ditches and banks constructed 1st-14th centuries AD. The earlier ditches belonged to a Roman fort while a non-Roman rampart was 5th-13th century. Finds included pieces of Roman and 13th century pottery. Maelgwn Gwynedd probably had a royal court here in the 6th century. A Christian ruler, he gave St Cybi land at Holyhead and St Seiriol land at Penmon. Rhodri Mawr ruled most of Wales from Aberffraw AD 844-878 when he inherited Powys and married into Ceredigion. By the 12th and 13th centuries the court of Aberffraw was involved with political and economic affairs beyond Wales. The last Prince of Aberffraw was Llywelyn ap Gruffudd, Llywelyn the Last, who was killed in 1282.

2. At the far end of the headland, on the eastern side, some stones may be seen protruding above the grass. These are the remains of a burial cairn of about 25 feet in diameter, built here 2000-3000 BC. This spot is also

a Mesolithic site – 7000 BC. It was excavated about 1974 uncovering many pieces of flint and chert. Some had been made into arrow tips and scrapers. Finds included two small axes which may have been used for cutting down trees. No bones were present but they would not have survived in the sandy soil. Some burnt hazelnut shells were found in a pit. In 7000 BC the sea level was lower than now, and the site was some distance from the sea, overlooking a river valley. The windblown sand dunes across the river have more recently filled in a large estuary, putting an end to Aberffraw's small port and shipyard. Today, from the promontory there are lovely views across Caernarfon Bay to the hills of the Llŷn Peninsula.

3. The tiny church of St Cwyfan was founded in the 7th century and rebuilt in stone in the 12th century. Since then it has been added to and restored but most of the church is 14th century. The churchyard wall, which surrounds the island, was built during the 19th century to check erosion. Watch for the incoming tide as the causeway to the island is covered at high tide.

Walk directions   **(-) denotes Point of Interest**
Starting from the car parking area on the east side of Aberffraw (1) cross the old bridge, which was built in 1731. Turn left along a track beside the river.

Where the track ends, take the coastal path behind a house. After 5 yards, turn left on an enclosed path that continues along the top of a wall.

The path descends to Afon Ffraw. Pass a white cottage and ignore a track on the right. Continue to a kissing gate.

Aberffraw church

Bear left to the end of the headland (2). Continue around the coast above rocks and a sandy beach. Go through a kissing gate and down steps to a shingle beach.

Ignore a path on the right which leads up some steps. Continue about another 150 metres to a path at the back of the rocks.

Continue above low cliffs and through a number of kising gates. Seals may be seen in the shallow waters or basking on small islands. In about 1¼ miles the path reaches the beach of Porth Cwyfan.

Continue around the top of the beach and follow the causeway to the tiny church on the island (3).

Return along the causeway and take a track that bears left uphill past a white cottage called Tyntwll.

Or if time is limited, return along the causeway, and turn right and walk back along the beach. At the half way point on the beach, there is a footpath sign which leads onto a lane. Follow this for a good distance until you reach the village of Aberffraw.

In about 800 metres the track descends and bears sharp left at trees near a house called Llangwyfanisaf. At this bend turn right through a gate.

Bear right across the middle of the field to a kissing gate beside a broad gate. Maintain the same direction to a kissing gate at a footbridge.

Follow the left-hand wall and enter another field through a kissing gate. Bear slightly left to a narrow gate at a footbridge. Slant left to a kissing gate and follow the left edge of the field to a lane.

Turn left and descend past St Beuno's church to Aberffraw village. Bear right in the square to return to the old bridge and starting point.

Facilities

Tea-room and toilets at the Coastal Heritage Centre, Llys Llywelyn in Aberffraw. Two pubs in the village. Ice cream van near the bridge during the summer months. Exhibitions and information at the heritage centre, open April to September.

Originally published in
Circular Walks on Anglesey

by Dorothy Hamilton

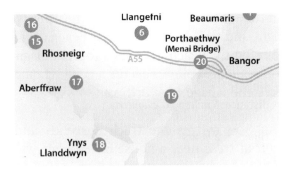

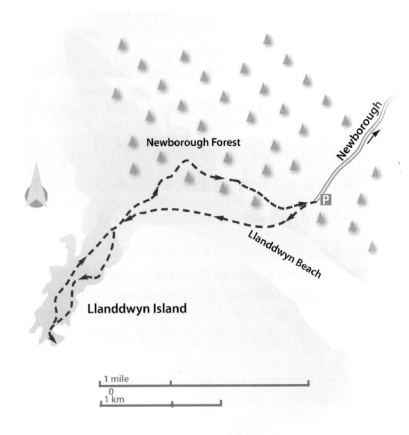

Walk 18
Llanddwyn

Walk details
Approx distance: *6 miles /9.6 kilometres*

Approx time:	*2 hours*
O.S. Maps:	*1:50 000 Landranger Sheet 114* *1:25 000 Explorer Sheet 263*
Start:	*Car park near Llanddwyn beach* *Grid Ref. SH 405 634*
Access:	*Follow the A4080 to Newborough, then turn left in Newborough and follow road through woodland towards Llanddwyn.*
Parking:	*Large pay and display car park with toilet facilities and information boards.*
Please note:	*Llanddwyn beach can be muddy due to the type of sand on the beach.*
Going:	*Beach, cliff and small tracks.*

Saint Dwynwen,
Patron Saint of Welsh Lovers – the legend
Llanddwyn, The Island of Lovers, is on the western coast of Anglesey, but it is not a proper island; it is a promontory sticking out into the sea. But at high tide the sea cuts Llanddwyn from the beach and it becomes an island for a short while.

During the middle of the 5th century a boat landed on Llanddwyn beach. In it were three young people –

Llanddwyn lighthouse and the splendid view across the bay

two sisters and a brother. They had been carried by the waves to Anglesey from south Wales.

The three were the sisters Dwynwen and Cain and their brother Dyfan. They had been living with their father, King Brychan, in a large palace – a palace which was full of music, laughter and dancing. One day, their father held a feast there and amongst those that had been invited was a prince called Maelon Dafodrill. Dwynwen fell in love with Maelon, and he also fell in love with her.

During the feast, it was announced that they had been engaged. Maelon could not wait to be married and he asked Dwynwen to return with him to live in his mansion before the wedding. But she refused as this would have brought shame on her family.

Maelon was very angry and he left the feast in a rage. Dwynwen was very worried about him and followed him into the forest although it was night and very dark. But she could not find him and she started praying hard, so hard that she nearly fainted. Then, in a dream God appeared and offered her a drink. She took the drink and immediately felt better. Also in the dream, she saw Maelon accepting the same drink. But he did not feel better, he turned into a block of ice!

Then God offered Dwynwen three wishes. She asked for Maelon to be thawed, for God to listen to her prayers on behalf of other lovers, and that she should never marry anyone.

She went home and told her brother and sister what had happened, and all three decided that they would work for God. The three found a small boat, went into it and left the wind and the waves to carry them far away from home. And that is how they reached Anglesey.

The three built churches on the island – Dwynwen in Llanddwyn, Cain in Llangeinwen and Dyfan in Llanddyfnan. These churches were originally built of earth and wood, later replaced by stone buildings. Since Dwynwen did many good things for people she was called Dwynwen (Dwyn the Good). Many women came to live on Llanddwyn Island and a convent was built here.

Dwynwen died on 25 January, 465, and the 25th of January is known throughout Wales as Saint Dwynwen's Day, similar to the English Saint Valentine's Day. When Dwynwen was about to die, she asked the nuns to carry her outside so that she could see the sun rise for the last time. She was taken to a rock in the north-west corner of the island. Suddenly, so that she could have a better view of the sun, there appeared a huge crack in the rock. And this crack can still be seen there today. At one time, it is believed that there was a well here.

The nuns in the convent continued with their good work after Dwynwen died and by the 14th century there was an important priory here with many visiting the place – especially lovers. In the priory, there was a golden statue of Dwynwen and pilgrims would place lighted candles at the foot of the statue whilst praying. They would also bring small white stones to be placed near the statue.

At one time, about two miles from Llanddwyn, in the dunes of Tywyn Niwbwrch, there was a well called Crochan Llanddwyn (*the Llanddwyn cauldron*). About a 150 years ago, there was a small cottage near it where lived an old woman who claimed to be able to foretell the future by watching eels in the well. Those that went there looking for a lover would place a handkerchief on the surface of the water which would attract the eels to it. The old woman would watch the eels, and by watching the direction they came from she could tell in which direction the one which had placed the handkerchief would find a lover.

By today, Saint Dwynwen's church is a ruin, but a service is held there once each summer. Towards the end of the 19th century, a cross was placed on the island to remember Saint Dwynwen and her good works.

The walk
Since the bus only goes to Newborough and not to Llanddwyn beach, you will either have to use a car or a bike to reach the starting point of this walk. Follow the signs to 'Llanddwyn' from Newborough. If coming by car, you will have to pay to come to the car park by the beach. Walkers and cyclists do not have to pay. Go through the forest and into the car park where there are toilets and information signs about Llanddwyn beach.

Llanddwyn beach

From the car park you will see a path going through the dunes to the beach. Go to the beach and turn right and walk along the golden sands to Llanddwyn Island.

Before reaching the island, you will see a small shelter with information on the island on it. Follow the path behind it going left through the gate. Look towards the rocks on the left and you might see seals basking in the sun.

Walk towards the lighthouse, but before reaching it you will see a large Celtic cross to the left of the path and the ruins of Dwynwen's church on the right. Continue along the path until you reach the Pilots' Cottages. Here there is

St Dwynwen's cross

Pilots' Cottages at Llanddwyn

an exhibition on the wildlife of the island – why not visit it?

Continue along the path and go left towards a small white tower. This used to warn sailors not to come too near the rocks of Llanddwyn Island. Now walk back towards the large white lighthouse. Go up the path and around the lighthouse for a wonderful view of the Snowdonia mountains. Now, go back down the path, and keeping left, go up a small hill towards another cross. This is Saint Dwynwen's Cross.

Continue along the path and back to Llanddwyn beach. After passing two large rocks on the beach, you will see a path on your left which goes into the forest. Why not follow this path rather than go back along the beach? This forest is home to numerous red squirrels – one of the few places where you can see them in Britain.

Beneath this forest are the remains of the old village of Rhosyr. During a huge storm 700 years ago, sand was blown from the beach covering the village and the

The remains of Llys Rhosyr

people had to leave. You can have more information on the old village by visiting the exhibition in Llys Rhosyr at Newborough.

Continue along the path through the forest until you reach a small car park. Then, turn left along the road and then right and back into the trees. Continue along the path, past a picnic area and information board with details of the flowers and plants to be seen in the area.

Keep to the path until you reach a gate and then you will be back in the car park where you started your journey.

Originally published in
Walking Adventures on Anglesey

by Dafydd Meirion

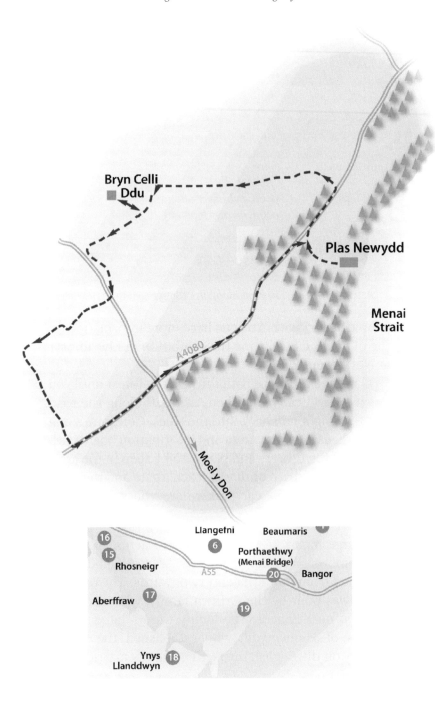

Walk 19
Plas Newydd

Walk details

Approx distance: *5 miles/8 kilometres*

Approx time: *2½ hours*

O.S. Maps: *1:50 000 Landranger Sheet 114*
                1:25 000 Explorer Sheet 263

Start: *Plas Newydd*
                Grid Ref. SH 518 698

Access: *A4080 from Llanfair Pwllgwyngyll to Brynsiencyn.*

Parking: *Large car park at Plas Newydd.*

Please note: *Farmland/fields can be wet/muddy, especially after rain. The path towards Bryn Celli Ddu is good, with a small bridge to cross.*

Going: *A walk through the countryside, with historical interest.*
                Take care when walking and crossing the main road from Plas Newydd at the start of the walk.

Plas Newydd

This large mansion, set in about 160 acres, has been the home of the Marquesses of Anglesey and their forebears from the 16th century onwards. The original house was built by the Griffith family, who also built Penrhyn near Bangor. The family were related to the Tudors of Penmynydd, who established the Tudor dynasty on the English throne. The family married into the Bayly and later the Paget families. Parts of Plas Newydd were built with profits from the Parys Copper Mine near Amlwch. The most famous inhabitant was Henry Paget who lost a leg at the Battle of Waterloo and was made the First Marquis of Anglesey due to his skill as a commander of the cavalry and second in command to Wellington. His exploits are chronicled in a military museum in the house. The house also contains a celebrated mural painted between 1936 and 1940 by Rex Whistler, a close friend of the family. There are also a number of family portraits by Whistler, as well as a selection of his work as a book illustrator, stage designer and decorative artist. There is a fine spring garden in the grounds and Australasian arboretum with shrubs and wild flowers as well as a summer terrace and later hydrangeas and autumn colour.

This footpath separates you from the main road

Walk directions

Park your car in the Plas Newydd car park (a bus service passes the main entrance and there is a bus stop nearby.) Go back to the main road, turn right and walk carefully, single file facing the traffic – some cars travel quite fast on this road. Go past a house on the right and then past a sign for the Sea Zoo, Parc y Foel Farm and Plas Newydd.

Go round the bend and then look for a footpath sign on the left. Follow it over a cattle grid and up the lane, past Llwyn Onn farm on the right to a well-constructed wall. Go left over the stile and walk with the wall towards the right hand side of a pine forest to a stile and gate. Go over the stile and across the field towards Bryn Celli Ddu farm. Go past a ruin on your left to a fence with a gate and stile. Go over the stile and towards the farm.

You will now reach a footbridge; don't go over it but go left following the fence and the stream towards two stiles and a footbridge. Go over and then right over another footbridge and follow the path to Bryn Celli Ddu Burial Chamber.

Bryn Celli Ddu burial chamber.

Go back along the path, over the footbridge and then right and follow the path until you reach the main road. Go left here.

Walk along the road, past a house on the left and up a hill. Go past three other houses and before reaching another two you will see a Public Footpath sign on your right. Follow it up a lane, through a gate and past a house on the right to Glanyrafon farm. Go to the right before reaching the farmhouse. Go through the gates and then left and through another gate and along a track to another gate. Go through it and along the edge of the field to a stream. Look for a small stile on your right. Go over it, through thorn bushes and then through a gate on your left to another field. Go over the stile and then along the right hand side edge of the field towards Cwr Du house.

Go over a stile and through a gate and to a track near the

After visiting the chamber, you will emerge onto this country lane, which will take you back to the car

house. Go left along the track up the hill. Go through a gate, a farmyard and another gate and out to the main road. Go left and once again walk single file facing the traffic.

Go past a house on the right and Llanedwen sign on the left and then the sign to Moel y Don on the right and back to the Plas Newydd car park.

Other Points of Interest
Bryn Celli Ddu Burial Chamber ('the mound in a dark grove'). It is the best passage grave in Wales. It started as a late Neolithic henge or ritual enclosure, with a stone circle surrounded by a bank and internal ditch. A later passage grave was built inside the ditch; the north-east entrance to the burial chamber is retained by a kerb of stones, which, along with the dry-stone walling of the outer passage, creates an elaborate forecourt. The narrow passage is 27 feet (8.2m) long and three feet (0.9m) wide with a low shelf along its north (right) side. This leads to a higher, polygonal burial chamber, eight feet (2.4m) wide, covered by two capstones. In the chamber is a tall, rounded, free-standing pillar, whose purpose is unknown. The spiral carving on the first stone on the left of the chamber entrance may be not authentic.

The whole passage was covered by a cairn, but the existing mound is a partial reconstruction, kept small so that three stones from the old stone circle and two other features behind the chamber, at the centre of the henge, can be seen. These other features are a pit (in which excavations revealed charcoal and a human ear-bone) and an upright stone carved on both faces and across the top with zigzag and spiral lines. The original pillar is now at the National Museum of Wales in

Cardiff, but a replica has been set up in its presumed original position.

The site was visited from 1699, and excavated in 1865 and 1927-31. The passage and chamber excavations revealed both burnt and unburnt human bones, a stone bead, two flint arrowheads, a scraper and mussel shells. Outside the entrance and the ditch, a small, unusual ox burial was found. On the ridge to the north of the site (on the right of the lane as you return) is a tall standing stone.

Moel y Don Ferries ran from here to the mainland at Y Felinheli from about 400 to 1850 when the Menai Bridge was built. Ships of over one hundred tons were built here towards the end of the 18th century.

Some say that the Battle of Moel y Don was fought here in 1282. Edward I's forces had occupied Ynys Môn and prepared to attack the mainland. Amongst his army were Gascon knights and Spanish mercenaries. A bridge of boats was built across the Strait and the army led by the knights started for the mainland. On the opposite shore, the Welsh were well hidden and as the English army started to clamber ashore, they were suddenly attacked. Panic ensued and the English were unable to retreat as men were pouring over the bridge. The boats started swaying and many knights – in full armour – fell into the sea. Others were cut down by Welsh arrows. Then the tide turned, and smashed the bridge of boats. About 30 knights, including their leader Luke de Tany, and over 200 English soldiers perished on that day.

Originally published in *National Trust Walks 1. Northern Wales*

by Dafydd Meirion

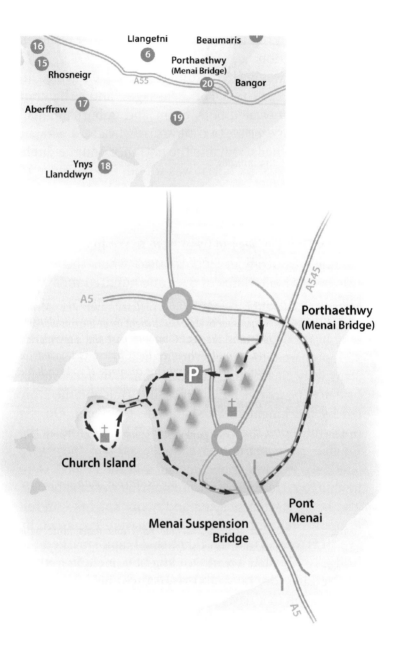

Walk 20
Church Island

Walk details
Approx distance: 1½ *miles/2.4 kilometres*

Approx time:	*45 minutes*
O.S. Maps:	1:50 000 *Landranger Sheet 114* 1:25 000 *Explorer Sheet 263*
Start:	*A large car park near supermarket on the A5, Bangor to Menai Bridge.* *Grid Ref. SH 555 719*
Access:	*Take the A5 onto Anglesey over the Menai Suspension Bridge. Go straight on at the roundabout, following the A5. Continue past the supermarket and, immediately after the Chinese restaurant on your left, turn left into the car park. If you reach the next roundabout, you have gone too far and need to retrace your steps.*
Parking:	*A large car park with enough spaces. There is a parking fee.*
Please note:	*Muddy path in the woods. Tarmac path everywhere else.*
Going	*Easy walking, tarmac path and quiet lanes with excellent views of the Menai Strait.* *Take care when crossing the main road to reach the car park at the end of the walk.*

Site highlights
- Attractive spot on the Menai Strait at water level giving spectacular views of the Menai Suspension

Menai Strait

Bridge and Britannia Bridge.
- Access to the Anglesey Coastal Path.
- Close views of waders on the mudflats exposed at low tide.

Walk description

This is an easy, short walk along the Menai Strait which allows you to appreciate the narrowness of the channel and the speed of the water-flow through it. Passing under the Menai Suspension Bridge gives you a view from an unusual angle of this spectacular bridge. With birds collecting on the rocky islets and exploring the exposed mudflats around Church Island, you can often get good close-up views of waders and wildfowl.

Walk directions

From the car park, take the right footpath beside the information board and follow this downhill through the woodlands.

Take this woodland path until you reach the Menai Strait

This rocky headland used to be common land, and signs of ancient civilisations here have been discovered as relics of Early Bronze Age cremation burials, Bronze Age axes and Roman coins have all been found here. The land was planted up as woodland by the Marquis of Anglesey who acquired it in 1814. It was then passed to the council in 1949, and opened to public in 1951 as part of the Festival of Britain.

At the bottom of the steps, turn left and follow the footpath downhill through the woods.

As you walk through the woodland, keep your eyes and ears open for Great Spotted Woodpeckers, Treecreepers, Jays and other woodland birds. This is also one place on Anglesey where you are likely to find a Nuthatch.

At the bottom of the hill, join the tarmac track and turn right, crossing the causeway out onto the island of St Tysilio's church. Walk around the footpath skirting the bottom of the island and enjoy the views of the Strait, the bridges and the birds.

The magnificent suspension bridge

At low tide, large areas of mud may be exposed and you are likely to see waders and wildfowl here. Little Egrets, Grey Heron, Cormorants and, in winter, Shags, are all likely to be seen on the rocky islets, while Oystercatchers, Curlews, Redshanks and gulls may be exploring the mudbanks. In summer, you may see Common Terns feeding over the Strait, and in winter, Red-breasted Mergansers can often be seen on the water.

At the far end of the island, a conveniently-placed seat allows you to sit and contemplate the Britannia Bridge, carrying both road and rail traffic to and from the island and mainland. You can also appreciate the racing, sometimes treacherous, tide through this particularly narrow stretch of the Strait, and imagine life in the solitary house situated on an island in the middle of this fast-flowing waterway. The path loops round the island passing the tiny church dedicated to St Tysilio, in the middle of its tranquil churchyard of slate headstones.

This church was built in the 15th century, though it is probably based on the foundations of a much older building. Legend has it that Tysilio was the son of a powerful ruler of Powys, Brochfael Ysgythrog, in the 6th century. Brochfael wanted his son to follow in his warring footsteps, but Tysilio wanted to pursue a religious life and fled here to escape his father, and founded his church.

Crossing the causeway back to the mainland, you can return direct to the car park up the tarmac track, if time is very limited. Alternatively, for a longer circular walk, turn right and follow the tarmac path round the base of the headland.

This stretch is known as Belgian Promenade, after the refugees who found safety and shelter here in Menai Bridge in 1914, and who built this promenade in 1916 for the community, as a way to express their thanks. Unfortunately the original structure had to be repaired after being damaged by flooding in the 1960s.

As you continue round the bend, you have impressive close up views of the Menai Suspension Bridge. Follow the path uphill past the steps down onto the foreshore. At the top of the path, turn right onto the narrow road and turn right again after a short distance at the Anglesey Coastal Path sign. The path leads you through a little beech clearing with standing stones of the Gorsedd Circle, commemorating the National Eisteddfod at Menai Bridge.

Although only a small area, the trees can be full of birdsong and you may have good close-up views of woodland birds such as Coal Tits and Goldcrests.

St Tysilio's church on the island

The path rejoins the lane and passes under the Menai Suspension Bridge itself. Continue along this narrow lane, past houses enjoying magnificent views of the Strait and the Bridge.

The swirling waters of the Strait have proven a barrier to invaders from Roman times onwards. A ferry has always existed here for centuries, and despite the difficult waters, a large number of ships used the Strait as the route to reach Conwy. The challenge was to build a bridge carrying the main London to Holyhead highway across this narrow strip, whilst still allowing sailing vessels to pass underneath. Thomas Telford was given this task, which he achieved by building the world's longest suspension bridge at that time, some 1,500 feet/457m long with its carriageway 100 feet/30m above the waters below.

Continue along this road past the bowling green and launching slip at Prince's Pier. Continue along Water Street past the marina and Liverpool Arms pub, until you reach the junction with the main road at Uxbridge Square in the middle of the village of Menai Bridge. If you turn right here, you will pass three cafés.

To return to your car from this point, cross over the road into Dale Street and turn left up the one-way road immediately before the former chapel, now turned greengrocer. Opposite is the film set for the Welsh TV soap opera 'Rownd a Rownd'. After a short distance at the end of this one-way road, cross over the road and take the footpath opposite you up through the woods between the library building and a block of apartments.

Again, although this is only a small patch of woodland, it can hold a surprising number of birds including Coal Tits, Long-tailed Tits, and even Jays.

After a short distance, you emerge onto the main road opposite the Chinese restaurant and the car park from where you started your walk.

What to look for ...
... in summer: Common Terns feeding in the Menai Strait.

... in winter: Little Egrets, Cormorants, Grey Herons, Greylag Goose, Shelduck, Oystercatchers on the water's edge, exposed mudflats and islets; Nuthatches, Treecreepers, Jays, Great Spotted Woodpeckers, Coal Tits, Sparrowhawks in the woodland areas; Buzzards circling overhead; Peregrine Falcons on Britannia Bridge.

Cormorant

... all year round: Little Egrets, Cormorants, Grey Herons, Greylag Goose, Shelduck, Oystercatchers on the water's edge, exposed mudflats and islets; Nuthatches, Treecreepers, Jays, Great Spotted Woodpeckers, Coal Tits, Sparrowhawks in the woodland areas; Buzzards circling overhead; Peregrine Falcons on Britannia Bridge.

Where to eat
There are three cafes in Menai Bridge. The first you will reach from Uxbridge Square is Café Aethwy, which serves hot and cold drinks and snacks, home made cakes and soup. Further on is Stafford House Fine Foods, a delicatessen which also offers drinks and snacks, and slightly further on again is the Castle Bakery and Tea Room, which offers hot and cold drinks and cakes.

Other information
- Free parking.
- No toilets at car park, public toilets in town beside bowling green.

What other sights are nearby
- Historic town and castle in Beaumaris.
- Penmon Priory and Penmon.
- University town of Bangor.
- Anglesey Coastal Path.

Originally published in
Birds, Boots and Butties – Anglesey

by Ruth Miller

First published in 2012

© original authors/Llygad Gwalch

© Carreg Gwalch 2012

ISBN: 978-1-84524-195-7

Cover design: Carreg Gwalch

Gwasg Carreg Gwalch,
12 Iard yr Orsaf, Llanrwst, Wales LL26 0EH
tel: 01492 642031
fax: 01492 641502
email: books@carreg-gwalch.com
website: www.carreg-gwalch.com

**Also in
the
series:**